Dreams
Dreams
Dreams
Dreams
Dreams

Dreams
Dreams
Dreams
Dreams
Dreams

Walter B. Gibson

GROSSET & DUNLAP
A NATIONAL GENERAL COMPANY
Publishers · New York

A Castle Books, Inc. Edition
Distributed To The Trade
By Book Sales, Inc.

Contents

Dreams
Dreams
Dreams
Dreams
Dreams

I

The World of Dreams

The question, "What are dreams?" has perplexed mankind from time immemorial. It remains as paradoxical now as it was then; perhaps even more so, because the complexities of modern life have drawn us farther away from the simple motivations that governed the dreams of primitive man. Any or all of our diversified interests and desires are apt to come to the fore during sleep and thus compose the stuff that dreams are made of, yet that in itself is a great advantage, for it gives us a chance to weigh one factor against another and come to some reasonable conclusion regarding our dream experiences.

If we could find a true Garden of Eden and populate it with happy, uninhibited people who had nothing to do but enjoy each new day to the utmost and fall asleep in happy anticipation of the next, they would still dream during the interim. Also, they would probably be more troubled by their dreams than we are by ours, for the simpler a person's life, the more it may be disturbed by an encounter with the unexplainable.

It once was supposed that primitive people generally enjoyed a deep, dreamless sleep, like little children. But modern studies show that even infants undergo a form of dream experience. In much of their sleep, eye movements are discernible and it is during such REM (rapid eye movement) sleep that dreams develop. Naturally, the scope of infantile dreams is limited; and so, to a considerable degree, are those of savages, because dream images are outgrowths of things that have been seen or talked about in waking life.

*9

Even in the deepest sleep, there must be some glimmer of consciousness, for unless the sleeper can respond to some sensation—either from an external or an internal source—it would be impossible for him to awaken. Thus an absolute sleep, if there were such a thing, would be the equivalent of death itself. Hence among primitive tribes, it was supposed that a deep sleeper had temporarily died; and in some cases, even a light sleep was regarded as a form of "little" death." Some modern thinkers have reversed this, classifying death as a "long sleep," thus linking the old with the new.

In the primitive concept, whenever a sleeper dreamed, it was proof positive that his soul or spirit had left his body and fared forth on adventures elsewhere. This notion has survived among many tribes until our present time, a direct carry-over from the era when such beliefs were practically universal. There are South American Indians who wake up from dreams of fishing or hunting and actually believe that their souls were so engaged. Some may even show resentment toward the headman of the tribe for sending them on long, hard journeys with no special purpose, simply because they dreamed it.

This belief in the reality of dreams causes other complications. With many tribes, waking a sleeper suddenly is a great mistake, as his soul may not have time to get back into his body. A native of a South Sea island was awakened in the midst of a dream in which he was in a canoe approaching a distant isle and he nearly went crazy, thinking that his spirit was still outward bound without him. After screaming frantically for his soul to return, he was finally quieted into believing that his soul had heard him and was coming back; otherwise, he probably would have died of fright.

Some Borneo tribesmen dread dreams of misadventures that result in a sudden awakening, because the status of the wandering spirit may be seriously affected. One man, for example, dreamed that he fell into a deep stream and was trying to swim ashore when he woke up and found himself back home on dry land. He was so sure that his soul was still struggling in the unknown stream that he sent for the local witch doctor to rescue it. There was a special procedure for such cases, so the witch doctor applied it. He filled a bowl with water and recited an incantation that attracted the spirit, which was logical enough as both the stream and the bowl contained the same element: Water. Then, with a miniature net, he caught the invisible spirit and carried it to its owner's body, which it promptly entered.

In some primitive circles, if a man dreams that he is in a fight, it is obvious that his spirit must have met up with someone else's and the outcome may prove quite important. If the dreamer wins, all is well; if he is beaten badly and wakes up feeling aches and pains, it is still a good sign, as it indicates that his soul has returned in that condition. But if he wakes up feeling fine, it can mean that his spirit was too badly hurt to come back, or may be trying to abandon him. That means another call for the witch doctor and his ritualistic remedy.

Among the Australian aborigines, medicine men have been known to chase wayward spirits into the glow of the setting sun and bring them back to dreamers who have lost them. This ancient rite somewhat resembles the resuscitation methods used by modern lifesavers who breathe air into a victim's lungs. In the Congo, the accepted method is for the witch doctor to chase the soul up a tree, spot the branch where it lodges and have the strong men of the village break off the branch, which is taken to the dreamer's hut and planted there. Gradually, by proper ritual, the witch doctor coaxes the soul back to its owner and all is well.

From time immemorial, these procedures have applied to illness along with dreams, but it must be remembered that many ailments are accompanied by feverish dreams and forms of delirium, so it all falls into the same category. Also note that whenever a witch doctor coaxes, chases or corrals a wandering soul, there is always a chance that it may get away, usually under circumstances where anybody might be blamed except the witch doctor.

To show how world-wide the wanderings of the dream souls became, we can cite the tribal customs of certain Alaskan Indians, who worked on a be-your-own-medicine-man basis. If anybody's soul was at large, they stuffed his moccasins with feathers and hung them up overnight. In the morning, if the moccasins were warm, they took it that the missing soul was home and they put the moccasins on the dreamer's feet. From then on, nature took its course. The soul went back into the body and permeated it, as it should.

Of course, if the moccasins didn't warm up, that was just too bad. But we have a lurking suspicion that they were hung close enough to the fire to make sure that it worked out right. That is, provided that nobody wanted it to work out wrong, which is something that can happen and has happened. As witness:

Among Malaysian tribes, it is believed that if the appearance of a sleeper's face is changed while his soul is off disporting in dreamland, said soul will not recognize its owner's body and will refuse to reenter it. Unless the situation is rectified, the sleeper will die; and at that, his chances are still bad, as the returning soul, if completely baffled, may have headed off for parts unknown. Accordingly, if one tribesman has a grudge against another and finds him asleep, his proper procedure is to smudge the sleeper's face on the chance that he is dreaming and his soul is elsewhere.

To insure this to the utmost, some connivers have been known to paint a victim's face beyond all recognition, even adorning a woman's face with a formidable mustache, to keep the dreamer's soul away. Others, however, have a simpler way of applying such a whammy. They wait until they catch the dreamer with his face upturned and his mouth open; then they lay a sheet of paper over his mouth. That does not disturb the victim's breathing, but it blocks the obvious route by which the absent spirit expects to return.

The question of what happens to a spirit that goes away and stays away has produced a variety of answers, one of the most popular being that it watches some other body until its soul takes off on a dream tour. Then, the first spirit moves in and takes over. As a result, some jungle tribesmen are worried whenever they dream, because they fancy that their village is surrounded by lurking spirits that are eager to pounce in and occupy somebody's body every time they see a spirit stealthily leaving the village on a dream prowl.

Much of this primitive dream lore was carried into early civilized beliefs. The ancient Egyptians spoke of a spirit entity called the "ka," which inhabited the human body as an etheric double that hovered near the body after death. Food was provided for the ka, which fitted with a primitive custom of luring back a wandering soul. But in Egypt, dreams themselves were often ascribed a divine origin, hence it was regarded as highly important to have someone interpret them.

Thus the Egyptians are credited with the first dream book, dating back almost to the year 2000 B.C., and preserved as a papyrus in the British Museum. It carried some two hundred listings, mostly of a simple, obvious pattern, which was understandable, as life was simple in those days and purposes were obvious. What bothered the ancient Egyptians most was putting themselves into a mood that would encourage dreams with significant symbols, whether good or bad. Evidently they regarded even a bad dream as better than no dream at all, as it would at least warn them of evils that might be due.

Methods of accomplishing that were recorded in other papyri, which have also been preserved. To obtain a full-fledged vision, it was necessary to appeal to one of the gods, since they were the recognized source of supply. One of the most popular was Bes, or Besa, the god of recreation, who gained recognition as an Egyptian deity about 1500 B. C. This required drawing a picture of Besa with special ink consisting of the blood of a cow, the blood of a white dove, frankincense, myrrh, black writing ink, cinnabar, mulberry juice, rainwater, wormwood and vetch.

Since some of these items are difficult to obtain today and their exact proportions were not specified, modern readers will probably prefer to test a simpler formula used for procuring dreams of a less visionary sort. No drawing of Besa is needed. You merely proceed as follows:

> Take a clean linen bag and write upon it the names given below. Fold it up and make it into a lamp-wick and set it alight, pouring oil over it. The names to be written are these: Armiuth, Lailamchouch, Arsenophrephren, Phtha, Archentechtha. Then, in the evening, when you are going to bed, which you must do without touching food, do thus: Approach the lamp and repeat seven times the formula given below, then extinguish it and lie down to sleep. The fomula is this: Sachmu epaema Ligotereonch, the Aeon, the Thunderer. Thou hast swallowed the snake and dost exhaust the moon and dost raise up the orb of the sun in his season, Chthetho is thy name. I require, oh lords of the gods, Seth Chreps, give me the information that I desire.

It was toward the year 1400 B. C that Prince Thutmes of Egypt took a nap in the shadow of the Sphinx, which represented the god Hormakhu, and like the neighboring pyramids, dated back more than a thousand years before that time. There, the prince dreamed that the great statue spoke to him in a fatherly tone, declaring itself by all its godly titles and granting Thutmes a long and prosperous reign, provided he would clear away the sand that through the centuries had covered much of the sphinx's gigantic body. When the prince became King Thutmes IV, he recalled the dream and ordered immediate clearance of the encroaching sand. An inscription was placed on the Great Sphinx, but perhaps Thutmes IV was too hasty. His reign, though prosperous, lasted only six years.

Whether that branded the dream as false, or simply proved the unreliability of the Egyptian gods, is open to conjecture. Many experts, ancient as well as modern, would agree that not only was Thutmes mistaken in accepting the dream at what seemed an obvious face value; he should have had it interpreted by someone else. There were contrary dreams that went by opposites, even back then; and many dreams that seemed similar could mean different things.

In short, Thutmes IV should have followed the example of another pharaoh, whose dreams were recorded in Biblical history. That king, angered at his butler and his baker, had them both thrown into prison. There, the butler dreamed of three branches, rich with grapes, that he pressed into the king's wine cup; while the baker dreamed of carrying three baskets on his head, the uppermost filled with cakes for pharaoh, only to have birds fly away with them.

Worried, the two prisoners call upon a youth named Joseph to interpret their dreams, which he did, saying that in three days, the butler would be restored to his position, while the baker would be hanged. Two years later, pharaoh himself was troubled by two dreams, both in the same

night, and sent for all his wisemen and magicians to interpret them, but none of them could. So the chief butler approached the king, and told him about Joseph, who was
promptly summoned to the royal presence to declare what
the dreams signified.

Pharaoh's two dreams ran thus: He saw seven fat cows
come up out of the river and feed in a meadow, only to
have seven lean cows follow them and devour them, yet
the appearance of the lean cows remain unchanged. After
awakening, pharaoh went back to sleep and dreamed of
seven fine ears of corn, all growing from one stalk; after
that, seven thin, withered ears sprang up and devoured
the good ears.

Joseph attributed these dreams to divine origin and gave
both the same interpretation; namely, that there would be
seven years of plenty in Egypt, followed by seven years of
famine. The fact that the dream was doubled gave it all
the more significance and when Joseph advised that sur-
plus food from the years of plenty should be stored against
the years of famine, the king not only agreed, but put
Joseph in full charge and the prophecy was fulfilled in
every detail.

It is interesting to note that these two dreams could be
classed as one continued dream, a type frequently experienced today; and that might have confused pharaoh's
wisemen if they tried to prolong its meaning and possibly
wait for more to come. Joseph, however, accepted it as a
recurrent dream, another type that has come under modern study and still is regarded by many analysts as having
special significance. Hence this stands out as one of the
most notable of all dream interpretations.

Equally remarkable among Biblical dreams was that of
the prophet Daniel, who was commanded by King Nebuchadnezzar of Babylon to interpret a dream which the king
himself had forgotton. Nebuchadnezzar expected his as-

trologers, sorcerers and other assorted wisemen to remember his dream for him; or otherwise undergo a process
of rapid extermination. Daniel, who was included in the
edict, arranged a stay of execution, in the hope that the
dream itself would be revealed to him through divine aid.
In due course, Daniel had a vision which he related to
Nebuchadnezzar who recognized it as his forgotten dream.

Daniel stated that the king had seen a great image with
a head of gold, body and arms of silver, belly and thighs of
brass, legs of iron and feet of clay. Daniel interpreted the
gold as representing Nebuchadnezzar's kingdom, the silver,
brass and iron being inferior kingdoms that would follow,
until finally, the clay, indicating weakness and dissension,
would hold sway, bringing ruin to all that had preceded it.

Such a dream would be regarded as supernormal by
certain analysts today, on the ground that clairvoyance or
telepathy could have enabled Daniel to envision Nebuchadnezzar's forgotten dream. This comes under the general
heading of extrasensory perception, more commonly known
as ESP, which in recent years has gained a definite place
in dream analysis. There are, of course, skeptics who
would doubt that; but conversely, there are Biblical
scholars who would still claim that Daniel's dream was
divinely inspired. The same applies in varying degree to
many other remarkable dreams recorded in the Bible.

In ancient Greece, dreams were interwoven into the
fanciful fabric of mythology to such extent that they were
originally regarded as the exclusive property of the feud-
ing gods, who transmitted them to mortals in order to
move them like pawns on a mammoth chessboard. Whether
the gods appeared as themselves or in the form of mes-
sengers or other dream figures, they were recognized as
the beings most concerned with the outcome of the Trojan
War or the adventures of the Grecian heroes, rather than
the humans involved.

The Greeks, however, also believed in oracles and as those increased in importance, dreams were relegated to a secondary place. So when the age of philosophy dawned, there was a trend toward rationalizing dreams. That marked the beginning of modern dream analysis, so a study of those ancient findings, in chronological order, should prove enlightening indeed.

A pioneer in this new school was the poet-philosopher Xenophanes, who came to prominence about the year 540 B. C. and charged the ancient poet Homer with ascribing actions to the gods that would have been disgraceful even for mortals. Xenophanes argued that whatever exists, must always have existed; and that all nature is a unity of which all parts must be similar. This was echoed by Heraclitus, known as the "weeping philosopher", who observed that in dreams, everyone retires to a world of his own.

Heraclitus summed this up in epigrams such as, "Man's genius is a deity" and "Character is destiny", thereby putting the blame for dreams upon the dreamer, rather than the gods. Heraclitus maintained that all things are in a state of flux, hence "there is nothing permanent except change." So it is obvious that dreams played an important part in his philosophy, though he appears to have regarded them as an effort by the individual to anchor himself in the mainstream of life, rather than be carried along by it.

Pindar, along about 460 B. C., came up with a double-pointed query which he personally answered: "We are creatures of a day. What is one? What is one not? Man is the dream of a shadow." From that, Pindar went on to claim that the mind in sleep is restricted very little by the body and could actually obtain better views of the future than when it was awake, though he added that all dreams did not come true. That opinion has persisted so strongly through the centuries that it sounds like a quote from a modern dream analyst.

Hippocrates, around 420 B. C., though inclined to see divine origin in certain dreams, recognized also that they could be signs of ill-health. Hippocrates is regarded as "the father of medicine" and though his contributions to that field were far-reaching and long-lasting, they were matched by those of his contemporary, Democritus, where the world of science was concerned.

Democritus was termed the "laughing philosopher" because he chided all men for their follies. In looking for an explanation of how dreams reached a sleeper's senses, Democritus decided that they must enter the sleeper's body through the pores of the skin. This meant that dream stuff was composed of particles so tiny that they were practically infinitessimal and therefore invisible. Once thus absorbed, they could be built into seemingly substantial creations within the dreamer's own mind, only to disintegrate in due course and return whence they had come.

This meant that they stemmed from the phantasms of visionary semblances of bodily forms which floated about in the atmosphere and attacked the soul in sleep. Granting these dream creations a reality of their own, Democritus applied his theory to the solid things of waking life. He assumed that an infinite array of indivisible particles, constantly in motion, were eternally contacting one another, thus forming a vast multitude of so-called physical objects which we mistakenly regard as independent matter.

Democritus termed these particles "atoms", thus putting himself a few thousand years ahead of his time, as witnessed by the dawn of today's "Atomic Age." He felt that life and thought were dependent upon these aggregates of atoms; that any sensory images were mere impressions caused by the more delicate atomic streams affecting human organs which were also of atomic origin. He admitted that there still might be gods, but if so, they were only larger and more powerful examples of the same phenomena. Thus accounting for everything in the world, he left no need for divine providence; instead, he set happiness as man's only goal, with dream life a way of attaining it.

From such, there grew a concept of one gigantic mind, of which the human race and all existing creatures or objects are simply thoughts, leaving the difference between the real and the unreal very slight. Plato, who came to the fore in the year 400 B. C., presented a graphic example of how dreams and reality might blend. He pictured a cavern wherein prisoners were chained throughout their lives, so that all they could see were the shadows cast on a wall by people and other objects that passed between the wall and the glow from a firelight, without ever glimpsing the real things. To this captive audience, such shadows would represent living creatures and actual objects; and they would be justified in considering the things that they saw as real beings. From this came the conclusion that all that we view in the three-dimensional world about us may be nothing more than such shadows and whatever else we take them to be is simply an outgrowth of our mind.

This could give our dreams the same reality as our waking life; or perhaps both could be regarded as pure imagination. It applies far more to our present way of living than it did in Plato's time; for through motion pictures we are able to see people who are dead and even hear their voices; while, through the medium of television, the same applies to events of the moment which are occurring as far away as the moon. Yet all these are but replicas—shadows, so to speak—and no more real than our dreams.

Plato, in reporting his discussions with his famous tutor, Socrates, presents other dream analogies which have a truly modern touch. He speaks of the governing principle of the soul as being mild and rational; but that when that reasoning portion is asleep, the part that is savage and rude, being satisfied with food and drink, accomplishes its ends.

"It dares to do everything," Plato wrote, "because it is loose and disengaged from all modesty and prudence; for, if it pleases, it scruples not at the embraces, even of a mother, or of anyone else, whether gods, men or beasts; nor to commit murder; not abstain from any sort of meat; and it is wanting neither in folly nor shamelessness." Then, after swinging to the opposite extreme in his dialogue, Plato sums up the initial statement by saying that, "In every one resides a certain species of desires that are terrible, savage and irregular, even in some that we deem so moderate; and this indeed becomes manifest in sleep."

Again, Plato was far ahead of his time, for this strongly resembles the Freudian school of dream analysis that was to become the vogue around 1900 A. D. The difference was that in Plato's day, people were apparently honest in their dreams. Whether their urges were divine or mundane, they dreamed about what they really wanted, at least on that particular night; whereas Freud was to see a hidden symbolism in what Plato might have classed as innocence. However, people themselves change with the times, so both men unquestionably had something to teach, each in his day.

Perhaps the man who had most to say for his time was Aristotle, who was tops among Grecian philosophers around 350 B. C. He dealt directly with dreams in three booklets and thereby produced a whole new school of thought. He attributed most dreams to impressions seen in waking life that were carried over into the domain of sleep. To back this, he insisted that there was no non physical world from which dreams could be fashioned; that is, there was no other recognizable form of experience from which man could gain the needed material. That consitutes a physical theory which has had adherents ever since.

However, Aristotle also believed that the soul was more sensitive during sleep and therefore could attune itself to outer impressions missed in waking life, thus giving it qualities of telepathy, clairvoyance and precognition that today are included under the general heading of ESP. He felt that physicians should give heed to the dreams of patients, because impressions that were crowded out of waking life then took over and were magnified in dreams to such degree that their meaning could be interpreted. This was the very essence of modern psychoanalysis.

The question of which is real, our dream life or our waking life—or for that matter either!—was by no means confined to ancient Greece. The Chinese philosopher Chuang Tzu, whose writings were contemporary with those of Aristotle, pointed out how one man will dream of happiness and awaken to a life of misery; while another, whose dreams are unhappy, will awaken to joyous surroundings. He stressed that no one recognizes a dream as such while it is in progress and he speaks of "a dream within a dream", which has become an object of modern study.

All dreams are included within the greater dream of life as we all shall know when we reach the great awakening; hence, according to Chuang Tzu, only fools believe themselves to be awake at present. In proof of this, he cited his own experience:

> Once, I, Chuang Tzu, dreamt I was a butterfly, fluttering hither and thither, conscious only of following my fancies as a butterfly. Suddenly I awakened and now I do not know whether I was a man dreaming I was a butterfly, or whether I am now a butterfly dreaming I am a man.

This dream was very appropriate because through the

centuries, certain Burmese tribes have not only adhered to the primitive belief that the spirit wanders from the body during sleep, but have imagined that it assumes the form of a butterfly. So any flitting butterfly might be a spirit that has lost its way, actually dreaming it is a person and apt to enter the wrong body just to prove it. If Chuang Tzu knew of this tradition in nearby Burma, he could very well have used it as a model to illustrate his philosophy of dreams.

Oddly, the ancient Greeks also had a "soul myth" regarding butterflies; and the goddess Psyche, who represented the human spirit, was usually portrayed as a beautiful maiden with butterfly wings, a concept that would link her with dream life as well as immortality.

When the Romans rose to dominance in the ancient world, they adopted much of Greek philosophy and adapted it to their own ways of life. Theories regarding dreams thus followed accepted patterns; but with certain notable exceptions. Marcus Tullius Cicero, the leading orator of the Roman forum around the year 50 B. C., wrote a lengthy discussion titled *On Divination*, in which he had his brother Quintus take the side of sibyls, oracles and dreams, stating their case in full. Then Cicero himself, in his usual analytical style, ripped all the arguments apart, branding all divination as "nonsense" and declaring that "dreams are not entitled to any credit or respect whatever," but belong under the heading of superstition.

However, Cicero was not adverse to playing an occasional hunch himself. When he dreamed that he saw the god Jupiter bestowing greatness upon a handsome young man; and the next day saw that very youth near the Campus Martius, Cicero decided that his brother Quintus might have something after all. Cicero learned that the youth was Caesar's nephew, Octavius, so he made friends with him. As Octavius rose to power, Cicero sided with him against Mark Antony, confident he would be backing a winner, which proved true. But later, Octavius and Antony made a deal and each agreed to sacrifice any of his friends that the other wanted. Among those fingered by Antony were Cicero and his brother Quintus, so the dream backfired.

After that, it seemed much smarter to take a middle course. Pliny, a century later, decided that dreams were of two classes, ordinary and extraordinary; one coming from over-indulgence in food or drink; the other sent by the gods. Here we have the prototype of a theory that is still held today; that some dreams are due to physical disturbances and others to psychic causes.

Then, as now, it was a matter of individual judgment as to what percentage belonged in one category or the other, meaning there could be as many interpreters as there were types of dreams. But the man who became the pacesetter for all time was Artemidorus of Daldis, who produced the most comprehensive dream book that had been written up to his time, about 150 A. D. He claimed that he had read all the existing works on dreams, that he had traveled extensively and had consulted or interviewed all the authorities on the subject wherever he went.

Artemidorus placed dreams in two overall groups: Speculative, which were somewhat direct in meaning, as they pertained to some immediate event; and Allegorical dreams, which required a few days or more for fulfillment, which even then could be opposite to the dreamer's expectations, since their significance was either veiled or symbolized.

One unkind critic took the attitude that the rules of Artemidorus were far from clear and according to them, any dream might signify any event and any interpretation of the same might be considered justifiable. But Artemidorus cleared himself quite effectively on that count, with the following statement:

> Dreams are proportioned to the party dreaming. Thus those of eminent persons will be great, as, if good, they signify great benefits, and on the contrary, great misery. If the party that dreams be of a mean condition, their dreams, with their events, will be mean also; if poor, ·their dreams will be very inconsiderable; for the rules of dreaming are not general and therefore cannot satisfy all persons, seeing that they often, according to times and persons, admit of varied interpretations.

Though this is still a bit fuzzy if swallowed in a single dose, it is easy to see what Artemidorus was aiming at, particularly in his last sentence. If times had not changed since those of Artemidorus, his findings would have become steadily stronger; in fact, they might have become so universal that they would have shaped many people's dreams, which oddly is exactly what has happened with some modern schools of dream analysis.

As for persons, when Artemidorus drew his contrast between eminent parties and those of mean condition, he was allowing for a whole range of levels in between; even including the chance that some one of high estate might suddenly become lowly, or vice versa, a common thing in the uncertain times in which he lived. This, too, has had its influence on dream lore and its interpretation ever since.

Artemidorus also listed dreams as having five different qualities. Under the heading Dream, he placed any in which the truth was hidden under some figure. A Vision was anything that appeared in sleep and later was seen in actuality during waking life. An Oracle was a revelation of a divine nature, coming as a dream. A Phantasy was a vain imagination, a carry over from waking life. An Apparition was a terrifying dream of nightmarish caliber, which some people would mistake for reality.

All these, with reasonable modifications, represent dream categories that are still recognized today. Taking the first group, that of bona fide dreams with hidden truths, Artemidorus proceeded to tabulate them in orderly fashion, beginning with each part of the body; then, the air with all its heavenly bodies; after that, the earth and many of its features. Each was very thoroughly interpreted and aside from a few that were highly fanciful—such as a person dreaming that he had three heads—most of the significations correspond with those found in dream dictionaries today.

II

Modern Dream Interpretations

During the centuries that followed Artemidorus, dreams came more and more into their own. Dreams and visions played a great part in the early development of the Christian church. Witness the Book of Revelations, which relates the visions of Saint John. It appeared shortly before the year 100 A. D. The early Christians regarded certain dream experiences as contact with a spiritual realm that could inspire their entire lives; and that belief was fostered and furthered throughout the Middle Ages and into modern times.

As a result, the interpretation of dreams was regarded as lawful and often encouraged, since any dream that proved to be of divine origin might carry a vital message. Even if they fell short of that, dreams were involuntary, which freed them from the stigma attached to ancient oracles and various pagan superstitions that had carried over into the Christian era. The line of demarcation was the avoidance of interpretations requiring sorcery or witchcraft. Also, there was always the chance that some dreams might be sponsored by the devil, so warnings were constantly issued against those.

Dream interpretation proved popular among Moslems as well as Christians, since much of the Koran was revealed to Mohammed in the form of dreams and visions. Though he had a monopoly on such revelations, it was still allowable to dream about the Prophet himself and thereby validate the remaining contents of the dream; and some of the Mohammedan sects developed into virtual dream cults.

Dream books of various sorts flourished through the centuries, but most of them were of Oriental origin and after printing was invented, many of those were translated into European languages and became the lineal forefathers of the modern dream books. They lost much in translati however, particularly when they depended upon w sounds or double meanings that were understandable o in their original language.

With the dawn of modern science, philosophers of Western world began examining dreams from a new v point. Around the year 1700, Bishop George Berkeley comfronted by the question: "If the things we see in dr life are just as real to us as those of waking life, hav any right to say that the material universe has any existence apart from our minds than our dream experi ences?"

Berkeley's answer was: "We have no right at all. The physical universe which I see, feel and infer, is just my dream and nothing else; that which you see is your dream; only it so happens that all our dreams agree in many respects."

When hypnotism gained recognition in the early 1840's, the full impact of statements like Berkeley's could be appreciated, for hypnotized persons seemed literally to be living in a dream world while apparently wide awake. In 1893, Dr. Thomson Jay Hudson, in his book, *The Law of Psychic Phenomena*, propounded the theory that man has a dual mind, consisting of the subjective, or instinctive mind; and the objective, or reasoning mind. Hudson came to this conclusion after a long study of hypnotic phenomena; and his theory was applicable to dream life as well.

One of the greatest contributions to scientific dream analysis was that of the French scholar, Alfred Maury, who began his experiments in the 1840's and continued them intermittently for nearly fifty years. Maury's work stands out because it was practical and direct, the sort that you can try for yourself and form your own conclusions, which will probably agree with Maury's.

Working on the "stimulus theory", Maury traced various dreams to their probable sources and then decided to provide the necessary stimuli to prove his point. There was only one type of stimulus that filled the bill; that was an outside or objective type. So Maury concentrated on that, with the following results:

Dream One: As Maury fell asleep, he found himself transported to Egypt, where he had been before and recognized by the general surroundings, which finally placed him in Cairo. There, he was in a shop owned by a man named Johann Farina, whom he had met there and who was now about to sell him some exotic perfumes in which the shop specialized.

With that, Maury awakened and learned what the stimulus had been. As soon as Maury had lapsed into sleep, a friend had opened a bottle of cologne, close enough for him to inhale it.

Dream Two: Maury found himself floating back through the years. He was a boy again, in the little town where he had lived. He was hoping to meet old friends, which he might have, because he did in other dreams. But in this dream, the only person he met was a doctor whom he had known in childhood and who insisted upon applying a poultice to the back of his neck.

Maury awakened to find that an obliging friend had begun pinching the back of his neck just after he went to sleep, prolonging each pinch to the point where the sleeper showed symptoms of annoyance, then easing it so as not to awaken him. This was repeated several times before Maury finally awakened.

Dream Three: Again, Maury's dream impression carried him far away to a past scene that he remembered well.

This time, he was in Italy, on a day so hot that he was wiping beads of perspiration from his forehead. However, the dream was pleasurable, because to offset the sweltering heat he was being served a bottle of choice white wine from Orvieto.

Upon awakening, Maury was disappointed to find no wine. The nearest thing to reality were the beads of perspiration. They were multiplied in Maury's imagination from a long drop of water that someone had carefully let fall on the center of his forehead.

Dream Four: Another hot day, with the rumble of thunder indicating the approach of a storm that would break the heat wave. But the dream retrogressed to an actual scene that Maury recognized; once again, he was vividly reliving the lightning flashes and the crash of thunder from a tempest that he had encountered while crossing the English Channel.

All because of a lighted candle, masked with red paper that was passed in front of Maury's face. The glow, reaching his closed eyes, had apparently first manifested itself as a sound, that of thunder, rather than its visual accompaniment, lightning. However, it is sometimes difficult to recall the exact order of certain dream events, just as with things that occur in real life.

Dream Five: Here, fantasy took over to a degree. Maury found himself acting as secretary for the Duchess of Abrantes, whose house was raided by an armed band of thieves. To make people tell where they had hidden their money and valuables, the invaders began torturing their victims by thrusting their feet into heated braziers containing lighted coals. The duchess arrived suddenly upon the scene and with that, Maury awakened.

This all resulted from someone bringing a hot iron close to Maury's face. The searing effect was sufficient to create a menacing dream situation, but since the threat remained constant, Maury apparently transferred it to victims other than himself. If the iron had moved closer, he might have thought his turn had come and promptly dreamed accordingly. Instead, it may have lessened, causing Maury's mind to visualize an interruption of the torture, as evidenced by the arrival of the duchess in the dream.

In all these tests, Maury relied upon capable associates to choose each stimulus without his knowledge. The application, too, was up to them, with Maury personally serving as the guinea pig in order to experience the results firsthand. Maury cited other dreams of this nature, but he also admitted to drawing many blanks. This in no way lessened the importance of those that did bring results; instead, it may well have been increased, since the dreams that were successfully stimulated stood out so sharply.

That definitely applies to the most famous of all Maury's dreams, which was the result of a chance stimulus that gained it the title of the "guillotine dream" and truly opened new concepts in the analysis of modern dreams.

In his dream, Maury found himself back in the French Revolution, more than twenty years before he was born. He witnessed sequences of violence and murder and realized that this was Paris during the Reign of Terror. He became so involved in the scenes around him that he himself was placed under arrest, imprisoned, and brought before the Tribunal. He recognized public figures of the period, listened to their arguments and found himself stating his case to his grim inquisitors, who remained totally unimpressed.

Sentenced to death by the Tribunal, Maury found himself being conveyed through immense crowds, all jeering at his plight. He reached the scaffold, mounted the steps and underwent all the ordeals of an actual execution. He was bound to a plank, tilted forward beneath the blade of the guillotine, which immediately dropped, struck his neck and completely severed his head from his body. With that, he awoke in horror, practically wondering whether he should be looking for his head or whether his head should be looking for him.

Neither course was necessary. Maury's head was still on his shoulders. It wasn't the guillotine blade that had hit him. A cross-rod had fallen from the end of the bed above his head. As he was sleeping face downward, it had struck the back of his neck at the very spot where he had anticipated and felt the guillotine blade of his dream. The result was that Maury had awakened instantly, yet despite that, he insisted that the stimulus was responsible for the entire dream from start to finish.

What a controversy that caused! Some scientists of that day accepted Maury's experience as proof that dreams happen in a moment, no matter how prolonged they may seem. Others insisted that there must have been a time lapse preceding the awakening, during which Maury made up the dream; or that he might even have elaborated it long afterward, when recalling it. Some even tried to show that the rapidity of mental operations in waking life is much greater than we realize, and that the same could be true of dream life as well.

One man, however, took an opposite tack. He assumed that Maury's knowledge of the French Revolution had so impressed him, as a scholar, that he had often dwelt upon its details and could readily have written an entire romance on the subject, with himself as the hero, perishing gloriously beneath the guillotine. However, being concerned with other matters, chiefly scholarly or scientific, Maury had never pursued his romantic trends further. Thus all he needed was an appropriate stimulus to trigger the whole fantasy into the seeming reality of a connected dream.

The man who noted this was a Viennese physician named Sigmund Freud and he promptly pursued his findings further. After citing Maury's other dreams as examples, Freud raised the objection that Maury's investigations traced the origin of only one element in each of his dreams—namely, the objective sensory stimulus—and that the rest of the dream-content was too independent and too full of detail to be explained by the lone requirement that it had to correspond with the element that was experimentally introduced.

"Indeed," said Freud, "one even begins to doubt the illusion theory and the power of objective impressions to shape the dream, when one realizes that such impressions are sometimes subjected to the most peculiar and far-fetched interpretations in our dreams."

This was quite funny, coming from Freud, whose own dream interpretations were to come under heavy criticism later. Freud's basic premise, however, was almost indisputable, as reading over Maury's dreams will show. Nor did Freud confine himself to Maury. Among many others, Freud quoted an analyst named A. W. Hildebrandt, as follows:

> In former years, I occasionally made use of an alarm clock in order to wake punctually at a certain hour in the morning. It probably happened hundreds of times that the sound of this instrument fitted into an apparently very long and connected dream, as though the entire dream had been especially designed for it; as though it found in this sound its appropriate and logically indispensable climax, its inevitable denouement.

This was Maury's "guillotine dream" reduced to simpler and much more controllable terms. To carry that still farther, Freud cited three of Hildebrandt's "alarm clock dreams", which ran as follows:

In one, Hildebrandt was taking a walk on a spring morning and came to a neighboring village, where he saw people making their way to church, carrying hymn books. He decided to attend the service, but waited in the churchyard until he became cooler. While he was reading epitaphs, he heard the sexton climb to the tower. Looking up, he saw a bell begin to swing and its notes rang out so clearly that his sleep was ended. But it wasn't a church bell that Hildebrandt head ringing. It was his alarm clock.

In the next dream, Hildebrandt was looking out of a window on a bright winter day and saw the streets deep in snow. He was going on a sleigh-ride but had to wait until the sleigh arrived. Next, he was getting into the sleigh, wearing furs; a foot-warmer was put in, but still there was a delay until finally, with a twitch of the reins, the horses started and there was a loud, familiar jangle of sleigh-bells that promptly awakened Hildebrandt. But the jangle proved to be his alarm clock.

In the last dream of the trilogy, Hildebrandt saw a kitchen-maid walking toward the dining room, carrying a huge stack of dishes, balanced so precariously that he was afraid the whole pile would fall. He called for the maid to watch out, only to have her retort that she knew her business. With that, the plates toppled and crashed in the doorway, waking Hildebrandt with their clatter. As the fragments faded, the sound became the ringing of the alarm clock.

The question was, why should these three dreams, all experienced by the same sleeper, under identical conditions as to time and place and with the same external stimulus, be so strikingly different? If Hildebrandt had been anticipating the alarm clock's ring or had recognized it in its early stages, his dreams might logically have been recurrent, repeating themselves over and over. The difference obviously involved some other stimulus, but there was no evidence of anything external other than the ringing alarm clock.

Thus, like the celebrated "guillotine dream", all these "alarm clock dreams"—not just three, but many more—

could well have represented a "meeting of the minds"—
subjective and objective—toward the production of a theat-
rical climax.

Working on the assumption that internal impulses were
the basic dream source, as opposed to come external stimulus, Freud fell back on an existing theory óf "wish fulfillment" as the primary cause. He pointed out that this was
often undisguised and recognizable, as in dreams of hunger,
thirst, or simple childhood hopes. But Freud kept on from
there, attributing all dreams to that primary cause.

"Wherever a wish-fulfillment is unrecognizable and con-
cealed," declared Freud, "there must be present a feeling
of repulsion toward the wish, and in consequence of this
repulsion, the wish is unable to gain expression except in a
disfigured state."

This gave Freud opportunity for some neat reverse
twists in his dream interpretations, but he explained them
quite satisfactorily, by assuming that "in every human
being, there exist, as the primary cause of dream-formation,
two psychic forces—or systems—one of which forms the
wish expressed by the dream, while the other exercises a
censorship over this dream-wish, thereby enforcing on it a
distortion."

In short, dream stuff can be classed as the product of the
unconscious, that portion of the mind that takes over during
sleep. Freud termed this "latent dream-content" and as it
works its way up to the level of the conscious, or waking
mind, it becomes "manifest dream-content" from which is
formed the dream that the person recalls later. But the
"psychic censor", as represented by the conscious, can alter
or even suppress any or all figments of the dream, unless
the unconscious manages to slip something by, often in a
disguise of its own.

As a striking example of slipping something by the psychic censor, Freud speaks of dreams in which a close rela-

tive of the dreamer dies, causing the dreamer such grief that he may even wake up weeping. According to Freud, this is actually a wish-fulfillment; in short, the dreamer wishes—or once wished—that the person in question should really die. To appease the censor, the dreamer either subordinates that thought or drowns it with a deluge of tears to disguise it as a dream of sorrow.

Thus the conscious mind is much like an adult reproving a child, the unconscious, by saying, "Naughty, naughty! You shouldn't do such things or even think about them!" The childish analogy is appropriate, as Freud himself stresses the brutal frankness of some children's minds, even in waking life.

"It is particularly interesting," wrote Freud, "to observe little children up to three years old in their attitude toward their brothers and sisters. So far the child has been the only one; he is now informed that the stork has brought a new child. The youngster surveys the arrival and then expressed his decision decidedly: 'The stork had better take it back again.' I subscribe in all seriousness to the opinion that the child knows enough to calculate the disadvantage it has to expect on account of the newcomer."

Freud used the term "id" to represent the portion of the human entity residing in the unconscious, thus representing the source of instinctive energy, seeking satisfaction in the principle of pleasure. By the term "ego", he referred to the part of the mind that reacts to the outside world and mediates between the primitive urges of the id and the demands of the physical world, thus becoming the organized part of the id.

In addition, Freud coined the term "superego" for a modified portion of the ego, which serves as the censor or conscience. It is the successor of parents or others who superintended the individual's early actions, so its chief function remains the limitation of satisfaction.

Call the Superego by its initial letter "S", the Ego by its initial "E" and designate the Id by a simple "X" and the three will spell S-E-X, which soon became the dominant force in dream interpretation. Being a primary drive, it came along with the id, continuing from birth on through childhood and into adult life. Thus in all dreams, it was possible to trace sex impulses back as far as infancy and encounter startling and somewhat shocking findings anywhere along the route.

When Sigmund Freud, like a plumed knight in shining armor, threw his gleaming lance full and fair into a dragon's nest of outworn taboos, scattering them to all quarters, the psychologists of the 1890's had nobody to blame but themselves. Their popular writings on dreams seldom mentioned sex. But they were largely concerned with the dreams of normal individuals, whose sex dreams, when they had them, required no interpretation. Rather, they resembled direct experience and the lusty dreamers of the gaslight era not only could explain their own repressions; they knew the remedy without consulting a psychoanalyst—if there had been any around to consult.

Of course there was one in Vienna, Sigmund Freud by name, and once he began probing deeply into the realm of abnormal dreams, he became so popular with psychoneurotic patients that he was able to confine his study almost exclusively to that field. He explored the minds of people whose waking lives were often filled with symbols that carried into their dream experiences, or vice versa. What was more, some of them were so sex-minded that they were swayed by Freud's queries as to their latent dream impressions to the point where they could very readily have concocted or imagined new dream incidents just for the thrill of proving him to be right. To Freud, at the outset, this was simply business, but as his findings were made public, they roused a whole new following, many of whom were eager to psychoanalyze themselves in accordance with his methods.

Unquestionably, Freud's contribution to our understanding of the inner mind and the dream world in which it dwells stands as a historic landmark. He began by studying dreams of all types and quoted many of them in detail, giving simple and direct interpretations. It was only when he began to recognize the deeper intricacies of the human mind that he evolved his more elaborate and perhaps fanciful theories which occupied his full time from then on and subjected him to servere criticism.

Dr. Joseph Jastrow, who was head of the American Psychological Association at about the time when Freud's findings first came into vogue, had this to say about their later development:

> To Freud, a dream is bootleg traffic in repressed desires. It smuggles its wares by wrapping them in camouflaged packages and employing ingenious dramatic disguises, at times with as little regard for the moral as for the logical properties. Unravelling the dreamwork, guessing the process from the product, tracing the primitive paternity and genealogy of the dream relations, is part of the art that Freud inaugurated.

As a psychologist, Jastrow contended that the study of dreams belonged in his field rather than the psychoanalytical clinic. Jastrow gave great credit to Freud and his adherents, but insisted that their specialized findings on dreams were matters of investigation for students of the subject in general. This is a very strong point, because Freud, as already stated, began his study of dreams on a broad basis, but abandoned it when he found that he could fit the dreams of many of his patients to patterns which he himself had shaped. Jastrow summed this with the statement:

What Freud does not sufficiently recognize is that dreams
do not all follow similar courses because dreamers have
different psychologies.

In support of that contention, psychological surveys of
thousands of dreams have shown that a majority could not
be interpreted in Freudian terms, except by what were
termed "ingenious and arbitrary assumptions or distor-
tions." Freud, in some of his own interpretations, spoke of
"distortion" in the mind of the dreamer, which it was the
business of the analyst to straighten out; so it is quite logical that it could work the other way around, with a dreamer stating a very clear and direct dream impression only to
have the analyst distort it to suit an interpretation that he
wants to give it.

Other surveys have often shown that dream symbols may
be the direct expression of some desire rather than an effort
to conceal it. For example, a man is invited on a weekend
trip, but having just recovered from an illness, he wonders
whether his physician would advise it. That night, still un-
decided, he dreams of two large ripe apples. He tells a
friend of the dream and the friend interprets the apples as
a sex symbol, by Freudian standards, as they represent a
woman's breasts.

However, the dreamer, in thinking back, is able to supply
his own interpretation, in this case a better one. The question of the trip, which would take two days, was uppermost
in his mind and he was determined to find a justification for
it, to counteract doctor's orders. Suddenly there flashed to
his mind an old saying, which he realized must have occurred to him in his dream, "An apple a day keeps the doctor
away."

So he had dreamed of apples, as a form of wish-
fulfillment. That also had a Freudian touch and so did the

proverb itself, for Freud placed great stress upon any play on words or bits of wit that occurred in dreams or were linked to them. In fact, Freud was very sure of himself, quite positive that he was right, and he was able to list cases in which his interpretations had worked out; and they will, provided that the dreamers are the sort of persons who fall in line with Freudian anaylsis. So don't sell Freud short.

However, Freud had his own problems with people very close to him and these had a very important influence on his interpretation of many dreams. Freud's whole theory of dream motivation could be summed up in a single word: Urge. One of Freud's early associates, Dr. Alfred Adler, took exception to the view and decided that the real answer could be spelled: Goal. Adler claimed that personal problems were rooted in an "inferiority complex" caused by handicaps, real or imaginary, which forced an individual to struggle for superiority. This meant that consciousness and unconsciousness moved together in the same direction, with no definite line of demarcation; hence evidence of the struggle would be apparent both in waking and dream life.

To illustrate this collaboration of consciousness and unconsciousness, Adler cited the case of a 40-year-old man who was happily married, had many friends and a good position, yet was suffering from one overwhelming anxiety, a desire to jump from a window and end it all. However, he never did, for in his own private battle, his striving to live and conquer won over his sense of inferiority and his desire to die. This, Adler noted, took place despite the fact that his inferiority was expressed in his conscious life and his superiority in his unconscious life.

Adler neatly summed up his mode of dream interpretation by citing two opposite cases: One, a student who was worried over an impending exam and finally decided that the time was too short and he would like to postpone it. The night before the exam, he dreamed of falling down.

Another student, proficient in his studies, never given to such excuses, dreamed that he was climbing a high mountain and awakened after gaining a magnificent view from the summit. This dream, according to Adler, reflected the dreamer's goal of accomplishment and represented his current life.

Going as far back as Artemidorus, there are recommendations that a dream should be studied two ways—forward and backward—in order to unravel it. Thus it resembles a mystery story, where certain facts are evident; others doubtful. Working from clues, the detective gains a different picture of what is true or false. Through this double treatment, the dream riddle can be cracked.

With that in mind, it should be easy to reconcile the views of Freud and Adler. Granting that urge provides drive, a goal should be able to direct that drive, giving the two factors a status similar to cause and effect. But Freud was so sold on sex as the one great urge, that he was unwilling to accept anything that might weaken or dissipate his pet theory. He insisted that any sense of inferiority would necessarily have a strong erotic basis; and intimated that inferiority was just another name for guilt. Adler, in turn, commented that dreams were first regarded by Freud as the fulfillment of infantile sex desires, with which Adler could not agree.

Not only did Freud and Adler fail to go along with each other's ideas, they failed to go along with each other. From then on, they went their separate ways with Freud adhering tenaciously to the Sex Urge and Adler emphasising the Drive for Power. Whatever the opinion of extremists, it is generally conceded that there is much to be learned from both Freud and Adler. The swing of the pendulum proved helpful to people eager to interpret their own dreams; for Adler was a strong advocate of some of the common dream patterns which have been detailed in Chapter III. Always, for extra-special interpretations of very unusual dreams, those same people could go back to Freud. So it was a case of "pay your money and take your choice."

Even more far-reaching, however, was the split between Freud and one of his later disciples, Dr. Carl Jung of Zurich, Switzerland, over that same old controversial subject, sex. Jung began his studies under Freud in 1906, and five years later bowed out to found a new school of his own. Jung took the view that Adler began where Freud left off. Yet each, to Jung's way of thinking, was deceived by a sense of finality.

Jung went along with Freud in recognizing the unconscious, on the basis that a dream gives a true picture of the subjective state while the conscious mind denies that such a state exists, or admits it reluctantly. But he also felt that dreams may mean almost anything; and that with an obscure dream, the first step was to establish the context, rather than try to interpret it. Inasmuch as Jung classed Freud as "an investigator and interpreter" and regarded Adler as an "educator", it is apparent that he valued Adler's opinions too.

Often, skeptical people ask whimsically: "Why don't experts analyze each others dreams?" The answer is, they often do; and that, quite curiously, was what led to the rift between Freud and Jung, thereby advancing a whole theory on dreams. They had been telling each other their dreams and Freud had not been doing too well at analyzing Jung's. That was possibly due to Freud adhering too closely to his "doctrine" as Jung termed it. Jung, who felt that more leeway should be given to the dreamer's own opinion, was analyzing one of Freud's dreams and asked for additional data regarding Freud's private life. This Freud bluntly refused, saying, "But I cannot risk my authority."

From that moment, Freud lost his authority altogether

where Jung was concerned. Rather than stay with fixed opinions, Jung preferred to follow his own line of inquiry, which he did, two years later. He eventually introduced the terms "extrovert" as representing a highly active, social person; and "introvert" for someone who is usually contemplative and satisfied with solitude and a quiet life. Jung took the term "libido" which Freud had coined to identify instinctive energy with the sex instinct and broadened it to include all forms of instinctive energy.

That expanded Jung's interpretations of dreams as well, so that in some circles he was actually classed as a mystic. As a result, dreams involving extra-sensory perception, or ESP, came within Jung's range of investigation; and the same can be applied to those with a religious significance. Interest in the work of Edgar Cayce, known as the "sleeping prophet" as well as other psychics, or spiritual-minded dreamers, has gained impetus because of Jung's broad outlook on the field of dreams.

Jung died in 1961 at the age of eighty-six and by then, extensive research was under way to determine the physical causes of dreams, or the factors involving the actual operation of the brain. For that purpose, scientists introduced a device used in Electroencephalography, in short form EEG, which until then had been utilized chiefly by brain specialists for diagnosing brain conditions. Through the EEG machine, by attaching electrodes to the skull, a rhythmic discharge of energy from the brain cells is traced on a photographic plate as a series of brain waves.

Experiments proved that during sleep, the rhythm decreased from Alpha waves, at ten to a second, down to Delta waves, at seven or less a second. This was correlated with breathing, heart beat, blood pressure and body movement, which could also be recorded by special instruments. Equipped for such tests, a sleeper looked like one of the earliest astronauts, ready for a space flight.

For every hour of quiet sleep, the brain and bodily action sped up for an average of twenty minutes. By attaching extra electrodes around the sleeper's eyes, it was possible to register rapid eye movements, as well. These were designated as REM and observers wakened sleepers during REM periods to question them regarding their dreams. Tests showed that better than 80% remembered dream activity, but when the same persons were awakened when no REM was being recorded, remembered dreams dropped to 8% or less: a mere one-tenth of the REM score.

Experimenters were also able to link these eye movements to things the persons saw in their dreams. A vertical REM might accompany a dream of two persons playing tennis. Naturally, some of these dreams could be traced to physical factors, with one person waking from a nightmare of being placed in an electric chair, due to the fact that he was all wired up for REM tests.

But the question of why we dream at all is still a subject for deep speculation, as our remaining chapters will show.

III

Common Dream Patterns

In all modern forms of dream analysis, the logical procedure is to classify most dreams as belonging to special types, thus making it possible to compare those that fall into one distinctive category. At one time, this was actually reduced to as few as seven such types, allowing of course for random dreams beyond the range of ordinary classification, or for dreams so uncommon that they required specialized study.

However, two factors soon became apparent: First, that many dreams in a given group had what might be termed "positive" and "negative" aspects—such as one dreamer finding money and another dreamer losing it—along with other shades of meaning that demanded broader interpretation; and, second, there were many "fringe" dreams that lent themselves to partial classification, but could not be positively pegged. Hence, by dividing categories and adding new ones, it was possible to define many dreams more exactly.

Here, the danger lay in broadening the groups too far, for once the process was begun, it was very easy to go on with it. Some psychologists have set the limit at twenty types, which is perhaps as arbitrary a number as seven. But at least it provides more scope; so we have taken it for the series of dream patterns that follow. At the same time it should be noted that the causes of each type of dream may vary, either because of conditions pertaining to the dreamer or the interpretation that the analyst prefers. But that in itself is helpful as it gives us a deeper insight into the vagaries of dreams themselves.

Falling from a Height This type of dream deserves first listing because it is often talked about and may become a subject of considerable controversy, although actually such dreams are comparatively rare. However, when they do occur, they are apt to be so frightening that they are seldom forgotten and some people live in almost constant dread of having another.

Usually, the dream involves the sensation of falling from a very high place, such as a bridge, a skyscraper or even an airplane. In an adult's "falling dream" the sensation is apt to be very realistic, with the speed of the fall increasing so rapidly that the dreamer feels utterly helpless and in the sudden awakening, the illusion of falling may persist momentarily.

There is a good physical explanation for this type of dream. Simply shifting one's body over the edge of the bed, particularly in a strange bed, or even merely sleeping in a strange bed, could account for a growing feeling of uncertainty culminating in a falling dream. Such circumstances should first be checked before jumping—or we might say falling!—to other conclusions.

If no physical explanation develops, the falling dream logically represents some other anxiety, such as losing anything from playmates, family or friends to social status. Careful analysis has shown that in many cases, this could mean separation from the dreamer's mother, much like a fledgling bird falling from its nest. That is a logical interpretation, strongly supported by the fact that many falling dreams occur most vividly in childhood.

Disciples of the Freudian sex school have tried to link "falling" with "fallen" to prove that such dreams show a loss of self-control as represented by a "fallen woman," who has dropped below the accepted moral standards. But falling dreams occur quite as frequently to men—and perhaps more often. So the main factor seems to be escape from some immediate dilemma, a rule which should be applied to women's dreams as well.

One very intriguing feature of falling dreams is an old tradition that the dreamer must wake up before he lands; otherwise, instant death will result. This, obviously, was intended as a jest, for anyone who died from the shock of such an imaginary landing would not be alive to tell about his dream.

Actually, there are persons who have felt themselves land after a falling dream, but they have never reported any impact, unless they fell out of bed. Then, the landing can be quite hard and even serious, particularly if the dreamer happens to be sleeping in an upper berth, or bunk.

Flying Through the Air This common type of dream has undergone great changes with the passage of years and therefore should be considered chiefly in its basic form. That takes us back to the last century when the only things that ever flew were birds, kites and occasional free balloons.

Freud, who was then coming into fame, favored the birds. Such dreams can develop from the rocking motion of the cradle, producing impressions of the stork winging its way above the tree tops, tying in with the legend told to children in regard to birth. Other analysts prefer to go along with a far more popular childhood character, good old Santa Claus with his flying reindeer, with room in the sleigh for anyone who wants to join him. Since the stork sometimes doubles for Santa Claus and brings Christmas presents as well as babies, both may be right.

Thus such dreams signify desire or pleasure, ranging from juvenile through adult stages, whether or not the dreamer will be able to attain it. But that in itself offers more definite prospects where flying dreams are concerned, such as an urge to free oneself from life's problems, not just getting rid of some people, but dominating them if need be. Flying, too, has been classed as a death token, with the dreamer taking off for heavenly realms.

Since most of these interpretations have acceptance, we can safely say that flying dreams depend greatly on the individual dreamers, the one common urge being to go places and to do things. But flying dreams do not include airplane trips, nor even an excursion in a conventional spacecraft. Those are the more modern forms of travel dreams involving anything from rides in hansom cabs through trains, boats and automobiles. They simulate an actual physical motion, rather than flying under one's own power and therefore should be covered separately.

Finding Money or Valuable Articles Some people dream frequently of finding money, jewels, rare books, rare stamps—or sometimes lesser items which they personally value—only to wake up with the imaginary gains fading from their grasp. For that reason, these have often been regarded as dreams of utter frustration; but that is not so. Rather, they are dreams of intense desire, which reach a state of temporary fulfillment, before they fade away. Which is better than what happens in waking life, when such hopes are dismissed almost immediately because the person can see no possibility of fulfillment.

Now comes a very moot point: Often, a dream of finding jewels, rarities, or even mere baubles, indicates that money is the real desire; because money is needed to buy those things. But when money is found in a dream it means that something else is desired, because money can buy anything else. That "something else" in the language of most dream analysts, is love, fitting with the old saying that many persons would do anything "for love or money."

Losing Money or Valuable Articles This is the opposite of
the "gaining" dream, but with different connotations. The
dream itself may be quite horrendous, such as losing anything from a bundle of bills to articles of irreplacable value;
but the greater the loss, the happier the awakening. It's
rather nice to realize that you haven't lost anything because
you didn't have it to begin with; but the dream itself may
denote a lurking fear of losing something tangible.

Some psychologists attribute these dreams to lack of
sexual drive or business acumen, as well as the desire to
be free of responsibility or a willingness to submit to someone else's authority. The noted psychic, Edgar Cayce, put
such dreams on a high moral plane, with the finding of val-
uables promising a reward through the development of the
dreamer's spiritual life; and the loss of some valued object
serving as a warning for the dreamer to avoid all pitfalls
that might lead to perdition.

Being Chased or Hunted These are exciting dreams, in
which you may be running away from a lion in the African
jungle, dodging a police dragnet in a stolen car, or playing a
game of hide-and-seek and hoping that no one will find you.
Anxiety is the common denominator of all such dreams, but
it takes on various aspects. Anything from an impending
business loss to a threat of physical violence can be built
into a monstrous creation of the dreamer's own imagination.

Such dreams can have a sex *motif*, based on the rule of
repressed desire. There is an old saying, applied to real
life, which goes: "The chaste are never chased." So it is
quite logical that anyone so overlooked in waking life would
dream of being pursued and even overtaken. Many dream
analysts go along with this, but Freud, the old maestro of
sex symbolism, takes an opposite view, as will be noted in
the next category.

Pursuing Someone or Something Pursuit suggests aggression on the part of a pursuer; hence such dreams can logically be attributed to an agressive urge of the dreamer. That may very well apply when you can recall something that you really want, and are looking for your chance to get it; but such situations are not too common. Usually, aggressive people are so busy pursuing their own desires by day that they don't have to dream about them at night. Also, the frustration element so commonly found in dreams doesn't fit with aggression, which is a very hard thing to repress. That is why Freud attributes these dreams to what he terms inversion, or "transformation into the opposite," meaning that if you are really afraid that something is coming after you, your tendency is to dream that you are going after it. That puts all chase dreams into the anxiety class, the dreamer simply being a worm that has decided to turn. Analyze your own dreams honestly and you may find out that Freud is right.

Impending Danger Some outside stimulus may be responsible for a dream where you find yourself threatened by impending danger; and the same rule can apply when other persons are endangered, so it is well to check immediate causes before jumping to more drastic conclusions. A danger dream of the drastic type may be just a step short of a dream in which the threatened person is seen dying or lying dead. Dreams of such death, by Freudian interpretation, have all the elements of a repressed wish-fulfillment. Fortunately, other authorities reduce it to repressed antagonism or even a secret guilt on the dreamer's part. So maybe you shouldn't worry about what might happen to people when you dream they are in danger. Instead, you should worry about what is happening to you.

Being Trapped in Tight Places This is frequently attributed to repressed antagonism or secret guilt, as with a dream of impending danger; but since it involves effort or struggle on the dreamer's part, it is wise to look for those factors in waking life. These dreams are by no means pleasant. You may find yourself getting jammed in a subway turnstile, or climbing up a ladder through a narrow skylight, or crawling through a cave that keeps getting smaller and smaller—unless it happens to be that you are getting big and bigger! When fat people have such dreams, they should look to their diet; but with other dreamers, the cause may be largely mental. Either they are trying to get out of some predicament or putting themselves in deeper, with no solution to either problem. Freud ties all this in with sex symbols, so they should be checked, too.

Missing the Boat The old phrase to "miss the boat" means to lose a real opportunity. So that, appropriately, is a standard interpretation of a dream that has been common property since the days when carpetbaggers rushed to catch a New Orleans packet and found the gangplank gone and the stern-wheeler ploughing down the Mississippi. When steamboats faded from the actual scene, dreamers began missing trains with steady regularity. Now that trains are fewer, people dream of missing buses or arriving at the airport just in time to see their flight take off.

Still, the same interpretation holds; that of a missed opportunity, but something new has been added. For one thing, if you manage to get on board just at the last moment and then wake up, it is a sign that your opportunity may come through. Often, if you think over your real life problems after such a dream, you may be able to peg the very opportunity that you missed and in some cases, you may salvage it.

That's nice to know, except that some modern analysts have concocted a different theory. They regard this type of dream as a reassurance against the fear of death. Since you've missed the boat, train, plane or what-have-you, it can't carry you away with it. Freud makes a play upon the word "depart" to uphold that interpretation. When a train or plane has left, it has "departed" and a person who has died is said to be "departed". To catch it and ride along without getting anywhere is supposedly a further cushion against the fear of death.

That might apply to some of the morbid persons with whom Freud dealt, but children, too, have such dreams. With them, a dream of missing a school bus might be a form of wishful thinking, rather than a dread of something that they may have scarcely heard about.

Interrupted Preparation Here, the dreamer may be packing for a trip, planning for a party, beginning a day's work, or a variety of other activities, always with the same result, the inability to get things ready in time. These are sometimes classed as a form of "missing the boat", since the same hoeplessness prevails. But often, these dreams are of a recurrent pattern, reverting to some former activity that the dreamer once performed capably.

Rather than connoting a lost opportunity, this may represent an effort to adjust to present circumstances and make the most of them. To have trouble with something that you did well in the past is a good excuse for mistakes that you are making right now. It can also be a case of banishing past regrets to allay future fears. People who have this type of dream frequently find that they have much in common.

Taking an Examination If ever a dream hinged on the individual dreamer, this is it. Obviously, a dream of facing a school or college examination might denote anxiety by the dreamer. When such dreams come as flashbacks during later years, they signify that the dreamer is confronted by real life problems, as with the original examinations. But here we encounter a paradox. Early in the modern study of such dreams, a survey showed that instead of dreaming of examinations they flunked, people dreamed of those that they had passed with flying colors!

Far from ruling out the anxiety angle, that upheld it. The conclusion was this: Faced by some impending issue, a person falls back on an earlier test that he met successfully. Subconsciously, an examination that he passed comes to the fore and he realizes how little he really should have worried over it. That, by sheer analogy, causes him to minimize his present anxiety. Freud attributed such worries to a carry-over from a childish fear of punishment for trifling misdeeds resulting in a constant dread of doing something wrong without knowing why.

This, in a real sense, resembles a rationale used frequently in everyday life. Anyone confronted by a new task ordinarily applies his present experience toward its completion. When it happens to go beyond his capacity, the old fears are roused, but compensate by magnetically drawing him back along the dream trail to a solution.

One man who had been driving automobiles for twenty years dreamed that he was having trouble with a driver's test that he had passed at the age of sixteen. When he awoke, laughing at his dream, he began thinking of a new job that he was seeking, depending on an interview a few days off. For the first time, he realized that it might be as easy as the driver's test that he had dreamed about, so he dismissed it from his mind and when the day came, the dream proved to be right. The job was his, almost from the start of the interview.

Freud went along with this form of interpretation, because he himself was plagued with examination dreams and his always had to do with history, the one subject that he passed with consistently high marks. He had skimmed through botany, zoology and chemistry; he had even flunked an exam in medical jurisprudence. But dream about those? Never! Always history dreams for Freud, when he was in a worried mood.

In fact, Freud was so intrigued by the way these examination dreams solved so many individual problems that he forgot to mention sex among them. His colleague, Stekel, corrected the oversight by declaring that such dreams referred to sexual experiences and sexual maturity. So Freud included that in his overall opinion.

Insufficient Clothing Here is an almost universal type of dream that runs the gamut from total embarrassment to outright exhibitionism, with various interpretations in between. Very often, such dreams are quite direct and free from concealment, literally as well as figuratively.

Dream analysts, however, have found ways to differ between the two extremes. Embarrassment, far from increasing in proportion to nudity, is apt to take the opposite trend. A dream of forgetting to wear the old school necktie at a class reunion might represent the height of embarrassment.

However, regardless of degree, Freud classes all such dreams as disguised forms of exhibitionism, a carry-over from an urge that was repressed in childhood. "Dreams of nakedness," announced Freud, in a tone of final authority, "are exhibition dreams." Other analysts have regarded this dictum as too thinly veiled. They interpret such dreams as a feeling of inferiority and perhaps guilt on the part of the dreamer. Edgar Cayce sees self-criticism in nudity dreams, with the dreamer's narrow-mindedness being exposed to his higher self.

But times have changed since the days of Freud, when even the most daring bathing beauties appeared in full regalia of skirt, blouse, stockings and shoes. Cayce, too, dates back before the era when bikinis took over as the proper form of beachwear. How well their findings would stand up in the untrammelled world of today is a subject for further survey. Possibly Freud's "law of opposites" would come to the fore with a member of a modern nudist cult suffering deep humiliation from a dream in which he fancied that he was even scantily clothed.

Water and Swimming From antiquity, water has been associated with birth, and this concept has carried into modern forms of dream interpretation. There was a myth of the goddess Venus emerging from the sea; and the Biblical account of Moses being found among the bulrushes of the Nile. The sun and moon supposedly rose from the River Ocean that surrounded the entire world. Streams were formed by springs that surged from the earth itself; and another Biblical account told of Moses striking a rock with his staff and causing water to gush forth.

Since those denoted origin or birth, it is not surprising that such symbolism should apply today. Yet water dreams were given many varied interpretations before they were finally identified with birth. The rite of baptism, whereby immersion in water represents a "new birth" might be classed as the "missing link" between the two. Indeed, the famed Edgar Cayce has defined a dream of baptism itself, as signifying a rededication of the holy spirit.

Other analysts may not go quite that far, but all will agree that a water dream is a search for something beyond the dreamer's immediate reach, or comprehension. They claim that the mind reverts to the moment of birth as the dreamer remembers or envisions it. This is much like making a new start on a difficult assignment, eliminating the problems of the present moment by going back to a time when they hadn't even happened.

In contrast, water dreams have occasionally been interpreted in terms of death, rather than life. The ancients spoke of drinking from the River Lethe, whose water brought forgetfulness. There was also the River Styx, over which the dead were ferried. The sun and moon sank nightly in the River Ocean of the West, while rivers themselves had a habit of merging with the sea. To cross a river means to reach the "other side", a term that denotes a life beyond the present.

To find a compromise between these concepts of past and future, some analysts have classed such dreams as purely mental, with the surrounding waters representing the limpid depths of the dreamer's mind, symbolizing psychic impulses. Conversely, some realists attribute most water dreams to physical causes, with bladder pressure a frequent factor.

Fire and Flame Like water, fire was regarded as a potent element in ancient times and therefore gained importance when carried into the realm of dreams. Sexual significance was connoted in the rubbing together of two sticks, to produce fire, which in its turn symbolized birth. Flaming torches, erupting volcanoes, added violence to the theme, which reached its peak with blazing funeral pyres and sacrifices of living maidens to the fire-god Moloch.

The survival of Shadrach, Meshach and Abednego in Nebuchadnezzar's fiery furnace, as recounted in the Book of Daniel, ran counter to such pagan rites, yet still remained a red-hot reminder of the torments of hell that awaited all who deserved it. Dreams of blazing pits must certainly have tormented many neurotic persons who accepted Dante's *Inferno* and other such descriptions at face value, but fire had its good points, too.

In moderate doses, it brought warmth and comfort, which made it welcome in dreams as well as waking life, provided it could be controlled. As one old-fashioned dream-guide put it: "Fire is favorable to the dreamer if he does not get burned." As long as that proviso was fulfilled, fire dreams were generally regarded as favorable.

But modern interpretations go deeper. Edgar Cayce injected a solemn note when he gave this analysis of a vivid fire dream: "The fire symbolizes the fire in self and is a warning that unless it is corrected, it will rend and burn you." One way to correct it is to put out the fire with water, which seems to work as well in dreamland as in every day life. The ardor represented by the rising flames is cooled by the surging water, or should be. But it isn't guaranteed.

Infantile carry-overs are found in fire dreams, based on the universal admonition given to children: "Never play with fire!" These furnish some interesting interpretations. As an example: A young man dreamed of stamping out a fire in the presence of his parents, yet awoke resentful because they had totally ignored his heroic efforts. However, the following interpretation explained the peculiar paradox.

The young man had been lacking in ambition, which had worried his parents. So to please them, he had made friends with people and was becoming quite gregarious by the time he met a girl and fell violently in love with her; but when he introduced her to his parents, they disapproved, quite as emphatically. So he decided to break off his engagement; and did.

That sacrifice carried into his dream life. The blazing fire represented the ardor of his passion, his stamping it out was his sacrifice to please his family and their indifference was exactly what he expected in waking life, but had hoped wouldn't happen in dream life. If he hadn't fallen for the wrong girl, he wouldn't have had to end the romance, so why should they stand by and cheer?

Given that interpretation, the dreamer accepted it so readily that he lapsed back into the original indifference from which his parents had prodded him. So nobody won out, except the girl who had become a foil between a misunderstood youth and his misunderstanding family. The correct interpretation of the dream proved lucky indeed for her.

Fire dreams have logically been classed as dreams of love, which they generally are, provided they do not go too far. Beyond a point, they can indicate an extremely dangerous desire known as pyromania. The lighting of matches, the wavering of candle flames, up through the fiery tongues that lick the logs in a fireplace, to the gigantic blaze of a roaring holocaust, all carry a fascination that manifests itself in real life as well as dreams.

How far some persons may go in putting those impressions into actuality depends upon the individual; but statistics prove that many arsonists have been impelled by such inner motivations. As with dreams of water, those of fire may sometimes be due to physical causes, so that factor should usually be taken into account.

Rescuing Someone Such legends as that of St. George slaying the dragon have been cited as evidence of the Oedipus complex, representing a male child's hostility toward his father, whom he pictures as an obstacle in the path of his own secret love for his mother. This seems rather farfetched, as there may never have been such a dragon, nor has it been specified whether the dragon itself was male or female.

The same Freudian concept has been attached to the legendary rescues of beautiful maidens, whether or not there is any opposition, implying that any young man who dreams he is engaged in rescuing someone should immediately class himself as a mama's boy who is willing to go to any lengths to prove it. Later analysts reduced all this to a symbolism, wherein the desire to rescue some-one represents a renunciation of something unattainable, in the interest of cultural advancement.

That settles the mother angle, and if any opposition is encountered, it is classed as an influence from which the dreamer must free himself in order to become independent, which can be construed as the father phase. So the dream, like a rescue in real life, is really a desire to save someone, who in this instance is probably the dreamer himself. When young women have dreams of effecting rescues, they are attributed to an Electra complex, which follows the Oedipus pattern but is considerably more involved.

Being Rescued By the rule of "transformation into the opposite," a dream of being rescued should be translated as a dream of rescuing someone. Granting that, the logical line of demarcation would be this: Where the dreamer figures as a rescuer, he is eager to gain independence through his own effort, regardless of opposition; while a person who dreams of being rescued may be depending on someone to pull him out of his present rut and may be totally unwilling or possibly unable to act in his own behalf.

These dreams have been given a higher significance by some interpreters. The dream of being rescued, in particular, is classed as a desire for spiritual attainment, or a hope of freeing oneself from present discord or depravity by trusting in some higher power. Most important, the rescue factor must be considered in relation to other dream elements, no matter which part the dreamer plays. In dreams of fire, water or fleeing from wild animals, the rescue factor may be secondary. Considering such components in their proper proportions is an important part of dream interpretation.

Being Lost This is a type of childhood dream that may crop up in adult life. When it does, its implications may be ominous. Actually, children are more apt to get lost while they are awake than dream about getting lost when they are sleeping, unless, of course, they are living in constant fear that someone wants to be rid of them.

That same underlying fear applies when some adults have such dreams and it may be that they are anxious to get rid of themselves. It is apt to affect people who have guilt on their minds or are afraid that undesirable acquaintances may catch up with them. It can even be that they are jaded with life itself. It is something of an answer to the inward thought: "If I could go and lose myself, how much better off a lot of people would be, myself included!"

In other dreams of this class, the link to childhood may provide the needed analysis. An excellent example was that of a young woman who dreamed she was lost in a quaint but unfamiliar city, with no possible hope of finding her way home until she talked with a fox that directed her along her way. That was the incongruity that enabled a keen analyst to solve the young woman's problem.

The setting of the dream smacked so much of an old-time fairy tale that she was questioned regarding those that she had read in childhood. Up popped the story of a fairy princess whose brother had been changed into a fox which could talk and guide people to the golden castle where the princess lived. It turned out that the girl who had the dream was estranged from her own brother and her urge for a reconciliation had caused her to picture him as the fox and herself as the princess in a tale buried so deep in her memory that it was all but forgotten.

Losing Some Necessary Item This differs from the dream of losing money or valuable articles as discussed earlier. Here we are dealing with another carryover from childhood, like the dream of being lost, described above. Children are always losing things or forgetting them and being blamed for it. Often, they have excuses and memory of those times may be responsible for adult dreams where excuses are in order.

But true to adult form, these excuses are somewhat subtle, in dreams as in waking life. If there is some place where you don't want to go, you may dream of losing your car keys, so you can't go there. Losing an umbrella during a rainstorm would have a similar interpretation. Dreaming that you are at a loss for words could be an excuse for not going to a meeting where you might be called upon for a speech.

Sometimes the items lost in a dream may be things you'd really like to get rid of, including people; but if you keep finding them before the dream ends, it may mean that you need them more than you thought. All in all, these dreams should be probed for early recollections, just like dreams in which you, personally, have been lost. Linked to such memories, they may bring up some surprising revelations.

Food and Eating There are about as many varieties of dream interpretations regarding food as there are likes and dislikes of food itself, including spinach. Certain foods are supposed to produce vim, vigor and vitality, with a corresponding increase in sex urge, hence some people dream of feasting on them. Others persons, plagued by dreams of such choice fare, have deliberately shunned it, as a form of self-restraint.

Dreams of gormandizing on a massive scale, far from signifying an honest hunger, are interpreted as a desire to eat up all opposition. That applies in a commericial way, which is bad enough, but when it becomes personal, it is worse. There are dreamers, we hate to state, who have actually fancied themselves devouring their wealthy relatives, which obviously signifies that they want to acquire the wealth of those wealthy relatives.

This is truly abhorrent, particularly to anyone who has no wealthy relatives to devour. It has been denounced as being cannibalistic, but really it isn't. The people who dream about it, don't really want to eat the people they dream about. They just want their money and why not? If they don't get it, the government will.

Diet also raises its ugly head where dreams of food are concerned. One man dreams of steps, each with a tray of a delicious salad containing the sort of thing that he is supposed to eat. He wakes up happy and eager to go ahead with it. Another man dreams of the same steps, each laden with all the wonderful food he can't have. He wakes up, wishing he was back in his dream life, making the most of it, rather than in the real world, getting the least of it.

In the final analysis, food dreams are always a question mark. People have actually gone to bed hungry, dreamed of eating a sumptuous banquet, and awakened fully fed. Others, contrarily, have dined heavily, gone to bed, and lived to wish that they hadn't eaten at all. The physical factor must always be considered where dreams of food and eating are concerned.

Teeth Dreams involving teeth have formed an intriguing theme since remote antiquity, probably because people worried about their teeth even back then. The precursor of all such dreams was the legend of the Greek hero, Jason, who ploughed a field and sowed the teeth of a defunct dragon in its soil. From that, Jason reaped a crop of armed warriors, whose attack he foiled by setting them to fighting among themselves until they had slain one another.

Since that legend still persisted in the time of Artemidorus, the famed dream interpreter of Daldis, it is not surprising that he should have translated it to fit his own observations. The sowing of the dragon's teeth meant the loss of a child's first teeth; the reaping of armed warriors, the emergence of the second set, which were firm and enduring through years of adult life until they yielded to the strain of their own champing and eventually eliminated themselves. Thus Artemidorus likened teeth to members of a family and to dream of losing a tooth signified the death of a relative or a close friend of the dreamer.

That interpretation gained increasing credence through the ensuing centuries, being fulfilled with more than average accuracy. As persons grow older, they worry more about losing teeth, while their relatives, also growing older, die off in increasing numbers. So coincidence alone can sway the balance in favor of that prophecy. Some modern analysts still recognize the classic signification, but only to this degree: They regard the dream as wishful thinking on the dreamer's part, particularly when the death of a relative promises an inheritance or relieves the dreamer of a burden.

Other modern interpretations include the hope of eliminating some pressing problem, which irks the dreamer like a troublesome tooth; or the anxiety of growing old, with an accompanying dread of death. Where younger and neurotic persons are concerned, tooth dreams have been interpreted to fit any problem, urge or fantasy involving sex. Just name it and that's it.

Or maybe it isn't. For almost invariably, there is a lurking suspicion that a dream of losing a tooth can be triggered by an aching tooth itself, with the pain dwindling as sleep continues, so that the real cause is gone when the dreamer wakens to wonder about it!

IV

A Master Dream Analysis

In the two fascinating tales written by Lewis Carroll, *Alice's Adventures in Wonderland* and *Through the Looking-Glass*, which are generally regarded merely as engaging fantasies written for the enjoyment of children, we find that the author actually probes deeply into the world of dreams, covering nearly every phase of normal dream experience. That is not at all surprising when we consider that in real life, Charles Lutwidge Dodgson, alias Lewis Carrol, was educated as a clergyman at Oxford, but turned to mathematics as a profession and became a noted lecturer and author on that subject. Even his austere writings carried a touch of whimsy and he was so intrigued by puzzles and chess problems that he gained deserved renown in those fields as well.

An important point regarding the two books mentioned, is that they appeared in the years 1865 and 1871, respectively, when the modern study of dreams was only in its infancy. It is possible that during the interim, Carroll surveyed the subject of dream life in greater detail, for—as will be seen— the original *Alice's Adventures* is replete with hit-or-miss transitions, while *Through the Looking-Glass* falls into a more natural sequence. But the fact that Carroll may have thought it out along such lines simply adds to the value of his findings as he subtly wove them into his intriguing narrative.

Another factor should be borne in mind from the very start; namely, that Carroll made the setting of the two dream stories almost diametrically opposite. *Alice's Ad-*

ventures began on a hot summer day, when she was dozing near the bank of a stream that flowed through a meadow and wondering if it would be worth the effort to go and pick daisies in order to make a daisy chain. Sleepily, she noted a white rabbit hurrying by and was astonished to see it take a watch from its waistcoat-pocket. Seemingly rousing from her dose, Alice followed the rabbit and from then on, almost anything could happen—and did.

In contrast, the setting for *Through the Looking-Glass* was in the dead of winter, when it was snowing outdoors and Alice was at home, curled up in a chair beside the fire in the family living room, playing with a kitten near a chess table where chessmen were arranged on a board. She felt wide awake and talkative, so she carried on a conversation with the kitten, telling it that she was eager to explore the room that lay beyond the big looking-glass hanging on the wall, above the fireplace.

Since only part of the living room was reflected in the mirror, Alice climbed up on the mantel in order to see more; and suddenly the glass was melting under her touch and she was going through it. She never realized that she had entered a dream state, for she still seemed surrounded by familiar objects of her home; and any fantastic shapes they took seemed natural enough, for they were in part the products of her own notions of what the looking-glass land might be like.

A striking point about Carroll's dream creations as he revealed them through the child-mind of Alice, was that they were quite uninhibited, which may logically apply to many childhood dreams today, despite the all-out efforts of some analysts to read sex and other complexities into every symbol or incident found in a dream. Possibly people were generally less inhibited in that comparatively simple world of a century ago and their dreams were witness to that fact. Or it could be that today, people are only interested in analyzing dreams that really disturb them and therefore disregard those with a whimsical pleasantry like Alice's. But it is not in the interpretation of Alice's dreams that Carroll's forte displays itself so effectively. Rather, he discovered and cataloged much of the fanciful stuff from which dreams are woven, showing time and again how things of real life—whether actual or imaginary—can be merged with dream settings and the characters that appear therein.

As the start of the original dream of *Alice in Wonderland*, Carroll recounted:

> Alice started to her feet, for it flashed across her mind that she had never before seen a rabbit with a waistcoat-pocket or a watch to take out of it, and burning with curiosity, she ran across the field after it and was just in time to see it pop down a large rabbit-hole under the hedge. In another moment, down went Alice after it, never once considering how in the world she was to get out again. . . .
> . . . . . .Alice had not a moment to think about stopping herself before she found herself falling down what seemed to be a very deep well.

Here Carroll goes into a dream sensation of a basic type, the "falling dream" which incidentally occurs much more frequently in childhood than is commonly supposed; and therefore was an ideal choice in this case, because he was able to stress it in terms of Alice's age level. With adults, such dreams can be frightening because they are fraught with calculated consequences; but not so in the case of Alice. Here, the falling dream was simply a continuation or intensification of her eagerness to learn more about the wonderful white rabbit, so her fall down the well was so slow that it frustrated her hope of catching up with him.

That, too, was typical of an actual dream and as she fell, Alice made many interesting comments regarding her plight, landing quite unhurt at the bottom of the shaft, as eager to

follow the rabbit as before. Here, Carroll went into a remarkable series of dream impressions. He had Alice find a
glass table on which there was a tiny golden key. She took
it and discovered a small door which the key unlocked, so
that she could look through a long passage into the most
beautiful garden that she had ever seen.

This was a case of projected imagery, as it it occurs in
dreams, for she couldn't have actually seen much of the
garden because the passage was so small that she could not
even get her head into it. Frustrated, she went back to the
table to see what else she could find there. As she set the
key down, she saw a bottle with a label saying, "Drink me"
—so she drank the bottle's contents and immediately dwin-
dled in size until she was only a few inches tall. Recovered
from that surprise, she was glad that she had now become
small enough to go through the doorway into the garden;
but unfortunately, she had locked that door and the key
was back on the table, where she could see it resting on the
glass top. But by searching under the table, Alice found a
cake studded with currants, spelling "Eat Me." She did and
immediately grew to a gigantic size.

Note the remarkable chain of hopes and frustrations
appearing in that sequence. Though they seldom fall in line
so neatly in the average dream, they are recognizable as
true types of dream experiences; and many childhood
dreams follow that pattern, though more briefly and ir-
regularly. But in recalling dreams and recounting them later, there is a tendency to smooth the abrupt changes, so
Alice's adventure was still true to form.

From there, the dream took on more terrifying aspects,
with Alice weeping so copiously because of her dilemma
that when she shrank in size again, she had to swim for her
life in a vast pool formed from her own tears. Here, Carroll
again introduced a primitive dream type, that of "water and
swimming" representing the wish that "none of this had evei

happened!" Instead of having his heroine waken, as frequently happens in such dreams, the author had her grow large again.

Next, she was jammed tightly in the rabbit's house, conforming to the "tight place" type of dream which also often results in an awakening; but instead, Alice was pelted with pebbles that turned into tiny cakes, which she ate and became very small again. Such transformations of one object to another similar in size, are also a common form of dream transition, so Carroll was still running true to form when he injected that device. Continuing the dream, Carroll had Alice meet a caterpillar seated on a mushroom. After reciting some nonsense verses, the caterpillar left, telling Alice that if she ate one side of the mushroom, she would grow larger, while eating from the other side would make her smaller, as desired. She tried this and from then on adjusted her size as needed for the dream adventures that followed. Again, Carroll had her finding her own solution to a problem, as dreamers often do, no matter how incongruous it would be in waking life.

Alice's further adventures included a veritable parade of half-real dream characters: A frog in footman's livery, a squalling baby that turned into a grunting pig, a Cheshire cat that grinned and finally vanished, its grin last of all. Others were a Hatter, a March Hare and a Dormouse holding a mad tea party in which they kept moving around a huge table to find fresh places. Getting clear of all that, Alice found herself back in the hallway by the glass table, where by proper nibbling on the magic mushroom, she was able to take the glass key, unlock the little door and adjust herself to just the size to go through the passage into the wonderful garden.

Such attainment of a dream objective often results in an awakening, as it is akin to finding money or some valuables which can only bring frustration when they fade away. But Carroll avoided that by neatly introducing new and effective elements. He had Alice meet three gardeners attired like playing cards, who were painting white roses red because they had planted the wrong rosebush by mistake. Soon, the Queen of Hearts arrived, accompanied by her court and after a transition involving a Mock Turtle and a Gryphon—both the sort of fanciful creatures that a child of that period could have imagined as being real—the dream scene turned into the trial of the Knave of Hearts for stealing the Queen's tarts, a situation straight from the annals of Mother Goose.

Finding herself in the midst of this, Alice was called as a witness, with the King of Hearts as the presiding judge. By then, she was growing larger, as she had before, and annoyed by the stupidity of the playing-card courtroom, she challenged them all, denouncing them as "nothing but a pack of cards!" At that, the whole pack rose and came flying down upon her; and as she brushed the cards away with a little scream, she awoke to find that her older sister—who had been reading a book while Alice slept and dreamed—was brushing away some leaves that had fluttered down from the trees upon her face.

Here, again, we find a masterful handling of the conclusion of the dream, the awakening and the ever-present question of just when one took over from the other, as well as to what degree. Here Carroll noted the factors which, at that time, other persons were only beginning to investigate, the working of an outside interruption upon the inner realm of a dream. In this case, it could be traced back to when Alice reached the little garden, which had trees of its own, thus setting the scene for falling leaves to be mistaken for playing cards and vice versa.

Now to proceed with *Through the Looking Glass:* This story presents a much more strongly defined dream sequence than the *Wonderland* adventure. Whether or not

Lewis Carroll had actually delved more deeply into dream analysis during the meantime, he most certainly placed more usable dream material at Alice's disposal than in the earlier tale.

As soon as Alice had gone through the looking-glass and found herself in the reflected room which until then had simply been the counterpart of her living room, she looked to see if there was a fire in its fireplace, below the mantel. Always, she had imagined that there must be one there; and there was. This was an excellent touch on Carroll's part, putting reality into the dream. Then, with that established, he had Alice find some chessmen lying on the hearth, which was reality, too, except that they should not have been there, because in the real life living room that Alice had just left, they had all been properly placed upon their board, so they should have still been where their reflection had shown them.

By having Alice accept that discrepancy, Carrol was able to let fantasy take over. Alice saw the chessmen walking about and talking to one another, which set the stage for further action throughout the story. However, her attention was temporarily diverted—another factor that operates strongly in dreams—when she found a book that was printed in a strange language, totally unintelligible to Alice until she was struck by the the bright thought that it must be a looking-glass book.

With that, she held it up to the very looking-glass through which she had just come and which had now resumed its solid form, making the dream all the more realistic. As Alice hoped, the mirror reversed the printing into English letters, enabling her to read a poem entitled "*Jabberwocky*," that still holds top rank as a masterpiece of nonsense verse. Now, Alice was really in a dream world, so she decided to take a look at the looking-glass land outside the house before trying to return to her own preserves.

What she found was intriguing indeed. It was summer instead of winter and when she tried to walk to the top of a little hill, she kept finding herself back at the house again, until she met the Red Queen from the chess set, now grown to life size, another typical dream fantasy. The Red Queen advised Alice to walk backward to reach her objective, another nice bit of looking-glass reversal. From the top of the hill, Alice saw a countryside with tiny brooks running across it and the ground between divided into squares by little green hedges that stretched from brook to brook.

Immediately Alice exclaimed that it was marked out like a large chess-board and added that there ought to be some men moving about it. When she saw there were some, she wanted to get in the game herself, if only as a pawn, though she admitted that she would like to be a queen. Her dream wish was granted and from then on, her adventures followed the moves of an actual chess game, which Carroll included with the preface to the story.

As Alice ran down the hill and jumped over a little brook, Carroll appropriately put her into a "flying dream" which carried her through the square of the chessboard that a pawn is allowed to skip on its initial move. During that flying trip, Alice dreamed that she was in a railway carriage with an assortment of odd creatures, but all that dissolved when she arrived in the next square, where she found a house occupied by the twin brothers, Tweedledum and Tweedledee.

These were also characters from *Mother Goose* and they were about to fight a battle as described in the nursery rhyme, but they were temporarily interrupted by a loud roaring sound which proved to be the Red King snoring as he slept beneath a tree. With that, Lewis Carroll introduced that greatest of philosophical enigmas, the ancient query as to which is reality, our waking life or our dream life. He handled it with rare penetration and skill, for without departing from his nonsensical *motif,* he introduced a thought provoking challenge, fit for consideration by a mind like Einstein's, yet still on a level that a child like Alice could appreciate, even though its broader implications were beyond her comprehension.

Carroll's passage ran:

> "He's dreaming now," said Tweedledee, "and what do you think he's dreaming about?"
>
> Alice said "Nobody can guess that."
>
> "Why, about *you!*" Tweedledee exclaimed, clapping his hands triumphantly. "And if he left off dreaming about you, where do you suppose you'd be?"
>
> "Where I am now, of course," said Alice.
>
> "Not you!" Tweedledee retorted contemptuously. "You'd be nowhere. Why, you're only a sort of thing in his dream!"
>
> "If that there King was to wake," added Tweedledum, "you'd go out—bang!—just like a candle!"
>
> "I shouldn't!" Alice exclaimed indignantly. "Besides, if *I'm* only a sort of thing in his dream, what are *you*, I should like to know?"
>
> "Ditto," said Tweedledum.
>
> "Ditto, ditto!" cried Tweedledee.
>
> He shouted this so loud, that Alice couldn't help saying, "Hush! You'll be waking him, I'm afraid, if you make so much noise."
>
> "Well, it's no use *your* talking about waking him," said Tweedledum, "when you're only one of the things in his dream. You know very well you're not real."
>
> "I *am* real!" said Alice, and began to cry.
>
> "You won't make yourself a bit realler by crying," Tweedledum remarked: "there's nothing to cry about."
>
> "If I wasn't real," Alice said—half laughing through her tears, it all seemed so ridiculous—"I shouldn't be able to cry."
>
> "I hope you don't suppose those are *real* tears?" Tweedledum interrupted in a tone of great contempt.
>
> "I know they're talking nonsense," Alice thought to herself: "And it's foolish to cry about it."

But it was far from nonsense. Carroll not only stated the peculiar paradox of who might be dreaming about whom, he gave it due elaboration. It wasn't just a question of whether Alice's dream was real; it came down to whether or not she herself was real. Even the two characters that she thought were real refused to admit it and with everything hanging on the Red King's awakening, the whole thing was bordering on one of those "dream within a dream" situations that present problems in their own right, adding that much more accuracy to Carroll's dream delineation.

Going on to the next square, Carroll showed further insight into the ways of dream life by having Alice find herself in a dark little shop run by an old sheep who was sitting in an arm-chair, knitting and studying her customer through a pair of large glasses. The shop-keeping sheep told Alice to look for whatever she wanted to buy and as she did, the items on the shelves moved ahead of her, so that every time she focused her gaze on a shelf, it was empty.

This, again, is a common type of dream fantasy that Carroll handled very effectively. Most people find it all but impossible to concentrate upon a definite object in a dream. From the shop, Alice found herself drifting in a boat, another recognizable dream occurrence; then she was back in the shop again, saying, almost in desperation, that she would like to buy an egg. The sheep placed one on a distant shelf and Alice started to get it.

That brought her into another square, where the egg had grown to such size that it proved to be another Mother Goose character, Humpty Dumpty himself. True to life, he was sitting on a wall from which he eventually fell and the scene became a turmoil of thousands of king's horses and men. In the square beyond that, Alice witnessed a fray between a White Knight and a Red Knight, which represented the White Knight taking the Red Knight in the chess game.

From there, Alice reached the final square, where she became a chess queen and found herself not only crowned, but seated between the Red Queen and the White Queen at a banquet being given in her honor. Naturally, that became fanciful, with a leg of mutton and a pudding coming to life, bottles and dishes taking off in flight, candles turning into fireworks and confusion reigning generally. Out of it, Alice found herself shaking the Red Queen, who was dwindling down to proper size and with that she awoke to find herself back in her own living room, shaking her pet kitten. That left her wondering who had really dreamed it all, Alice herself or the Red King.

Along with his remarkable handling of dream sequences and transitions in both *Alice's Adventures in Wonderland* and *Through the Looking-Glass*, the author introduced many appropriate and deep-reaching features. Birds and animals talked throughout the tales, whenever they had occasion or reason to do so; and at times, flowers talked as well. That is in keeping with many recorded dream experiences and was particularly apt in a childhood dream.

Like all dreams, those of childhood are often based on previous experience, which in childhood—particularly in Carroll's day—tied in strongly with fairy tales as well as nursery rhymes. In fairy tales, creatures and even flowers talk. A child, conditioned to such a premise, would logically find a realization of such hopes in a dream adventure, as Alice did. Carroll also introduced mythical creatures, such as the Gryphon and synthetic creatures, as the Mock Turtle, just because of their appeal to childish minds. The Mock Turtle was indeed a fine touch, for in those days, mock turtle soup—an imitation of the genuine article—was a frequent prelude to a family dinner and children could very well believed that there was such an animal as the Mock Turtle.

This makes it sound as though Carroll's "Alice" was a real person, which she was. Her full name was Alice Pleasance Liddell and she was the eldest of three sisters to whom

Carroll told the first *Wonderland* tale, making her the heroine and saying that she would live many long years to remember it, which she did; for she was in her eighties when she visited America and received a doctorate at Columbia University.

But the real touch came at the end of *Through the Looking-Glass*, where Carroll added a twenty-one line poem, which practially nobody reads, but which everybody should read, particularly the first three lines and the last three.

> A boat, beneath a sunny sky
> Lingering onward dreamily
> In an evening of July—
> * * * * * * * * * *
>
> Ever drifting down the stream—
> Lingering in the golden gleam—
> Life, what is it but a dream?

With that, Lewis Carroll summed it up just about as well as any philosophers or psychologists ever did before—or since.

V

Remarkable Psychic Dreams

The dreams comprising this chapter could very well be classed as "predictive" and "projective" because in each case, there was some warning of a threatening disaster, or the dreamer found himself transported to some other scene. It will be noted that each dreamer recognized his surroundings and that they had to with something of importance to himself.

Many times, people dream of something more or less familiar, but seldom are the scenes so sharply etched as they were in these dreams. Also, in these cases, the events fell into a logical sequence, as they would in real life. Therefore, their significance far transcends anything resembling mere coincidence, yet at the same time, they could have been the product of the dreamer's own imagination, brought to a stage of vivid realism.

That, in turn, shows the power of the inner mind to envision the unseen, whether it relates to past, present or future. Yet amazing though such dreams may seem, they are by no means as rare as is generally supposed. For every dream of this type that is recorded, a dozen may be overlooked, simply because their potential significance was not recognized at the time of their occurrence, or they seemed too fantastic to be true.

So keep track of your dreams or any that are told to you. For all you now know, they may be predictions in the making!

Mark Twain's Dream When Mark Twain was a cub pilot on

the Mississippi, his younger brother Henry was working as an apprentice clerk on the same steamboat, the *Pennsylvania.* While the boat was laying in port at St. Louis, they stayed at the home of their sister, Pamela Moffett, whose husband was a prosperous merchant in that city.

On the last night, Henry went back to the boat, but Mark Twain slept at the house and in the morning awakened from a dream so vivid that he fully believed that it was real. It was the type involving his immediate surroundings, the kind that are so hard to shake off, and this one was particularly harrowing. He dreamed that he saw a metal casket resting upon two chairs in the family sitting room. In it lay his brother Henry, wearing an old suit belonging to Mark Twain and on Henry's body was a wreath of white roses , with a red one in the center.

How and when Henry had died, Mark Twain could not recall, which made it all the more difficult for him to face the family, particularly his mother, who was staying at his sister's home. So he dressed and stole quietly downstairs and out of the house, without daring to look into that room where he was so sure that Henry's body lay, so vividly had he seen it. Only when he was a block or more away did Mark Twain realize that the whole thing was a dream, so he hurried back and found the sitting room in its accustomed order: No casket, no body, no roses, not even the two chairs.

Mark Twain said nothing to his brother about the dream, but when the *Pennsylvania* reached New Orleans, he switched to another packet and when they parted company, he gave Henry a serious talk on how to handle himself in case of a steamboat explosion. There was nothing precognitive in that; if Mark Twain had really expected the *Pennsylvania* to blow up, he would have told Henry to forget the river and take a job on shore.

But the *Pennsylvania* did blow up a few days later near Memphis and when Mark Twain reached that city on another boat, the *A. T. Lacey*, he found Henry among the desperately injured in an improvised hospital. Henry rallied briefly, but died on the sixth night and when Mark Twain came to see the body, his grief was coupled with amazement. All the previous victims had been placed in wooden coffins, but some ladies of Memphis had provided a metal casket for Henry, exactly like the one that Mark Twain had seen in his dreams!

Moreover, Henry was attired in a suit that had belonged to Mark Twain, who stared in disbelief, realizing that the only missing detail was the flowers. As his mind went back to that, a lady entered the dead room, approached the casket and placed a floral wreath on Henry's body. It consisted of white roses with a red rose in the center.

That was not all. When Mark Twain brought the body to to St. Louis, he went to his brother-in-law's place of business, but missed him because he was on his way to the boat. So Mark Twain went to the house, arriving there just as some men were unloading the casket from a wagon. Upstairs, in the very sitting room that Mark Twain had dreamed about, were the same two chairs, set to receive it, also in exact keeping with his dream!

The Coronation Dream A singular case of an apparently recurrent dream with a decidedly ominous touch was reported at the time of the Coronation of King Edward VII of England, in 1902. Early in June, the ceremony was set for the 26th of the month and the Duke of Portland, who held the high official rank of Master of the Horse, took charge of arrangements for the coronation procession.

Though that involved many details, the basic pattern was simple enough as the procession was to follow the traditional route, which was last used by Queen Victoria, some sixty-four years before. The Duke of Portland checked that out, found it quite satisfactory and then devoted his attention to other details, all of a more modern and more pressing nature. That was when he had his dream.

In his dream, the duke saw the crown that topped the royal coach topple from its perch. He was so impressed by the dream that he inspected the old royal coach and found the crown firmly fixed. He examined the wheels and all the rest, to find everything in order. Nothing, it seemed, could possibly trouble the royal coach along that route.

So when the duke had another similar dream, he began to see a symbolism in it. The king himself might be endangered, perhaps the monarchy as well. Then, suddenly, the king became seriously ill, confirming that impression. With only two days to go, the Coronation was postponed, not to the duke's relief, but to his fear that it might never be held, as the dream could have presaged the king's death.

Instead, King Edward recovered rapidly and the coronation was set for August 9th, which pleased everybody except the Duke of Portland, because he had the same dream again, more vividly than before. The crown toppling from the top of the coach could mean that the king could suffer a relapse and there would never be a coronation of Edward VII, King of England.

Picture the duke's dilemma. Should he talk to the king and warn him of the premonition? That would be bad, in fact very bad. The king's physicians had decided that he would be well enough to go through with the Coronation, but even they were pressing it as something immediate, which brooked no interference. Even to suggest some problem might provoke the very relapse that the duke feared.

So the Duke of Portland concentrated on the matter of the coach itself, perhaps on the assumption that he personally might be more deeply involved than the king. If the dream concerned the royal coach, that could produce problems for the duke himself, as Master of the Horse. So the proper thing was to make another check of the route that the coach was to follow.

The duke did exactly that and came to the Horse Guard's Arch, under which the royal coach had always passed with room to spare. But when he had it measured, just to make sure, it proved to be a foot or more too short. Which meant that:

If the coronation procession had taken place as planned, the crown that topped the royal coach would have crashed into the archway and would have toppled down, just as in the dream!

But why?

The royal coach had gone through that same archway, time and again, without any problem. But "time and again" was in itself a misnomer. Times between coronations had been shorter, a century and more ago. People had lived more slowly, with less changes and less cares, back in those days. Modern improvements, such as better paving, had not even been considered, even as late as the time of Queen Victoria's Coronation, which after all, had been held sixty-four years ago.

So the Duke of Portland found the answer to his problem, through a dream. During those sixty-four years, the London streets had been repaved with increasing frequency. Inch by inch, inches by inches, the roadway under the Horse Guard's Arch had worked upward without anyone realizing it, until the archway itself was too low to accomodate the royal coach!

That was properly rectified. There wasn't time to lower the roadway or raise the arch. But it was simple to alter the royal coach by bringing the crown down just enough so that it could pass through, coach and all, with no problem. So that was done and the Coronation of Edward VII went through as scheduled, thanks to the heeding of a warning from a dream.

This dream can be classed as a prophetic type, since it

was a portent of what would have happened if its warning had been ignored. More strictly, it could be typed as an intuitive dream. The duke, in going over the route, could have sensed that the arch was too low, but had dismissed the notion because of its recorded measurements. Later, the same inner impression recurred in dream form as it might actually have happened.

The Rings of Ninib If a dream can carry the dreamer into the far distant future, enabling him to bring back reports of the world-to-be, there is no good reason why he should not be conveyed back into the very remote past, to find out something about the world-that-was. Oddly, there are far more "past" dreams than "future" dreams, because they hinge on the known rather than the unknown.

But since we already know about the past, it doesn't hold much interest, unless something startlingly new is revealed regarding it. Hence, though many such dreams have been recorded, few have gained the recognition that they have rightfully deserved. Here is one of the few:

Early in the year 1893, Dr. Herman V. Hilprecht, Professor of Assyrian at the University of Pennsylvania, was trying to decipher the inscriptions on two earrings made of agate that had been unearthed by the University's Expedition to Nippur, near the site of ancient Babylon. To make it really difficult, all that Dr. Hilprecht had to work with were sketches of the rings and not the rings themselves. At last, toward midnight, he gave it up and decided to get some sleep, wishing that he could be there in the Asiatic desert by the drab mounds of ancient Nippur, to see what else he might dig up to help him in his thankless task.

Hilprecht's wish came true in dream form, but beyond all his expectations. Instead of finding himself among the ruins, he dreamed that he was in ancient Nippur itself. There, he was greeted by an ancient Assyrian priest, who conducted him through a fabulous temple to a treasure chamber, where he saw beautiful specimens of agate and lapis lazuli, a gem stone resembling sapphire.

There, the priest told him that he had been ordered to make a pair of agate ear rings for the statue of Ninib, son of the great god Bel, but the only available material was a votive cylinder that had been offered to Bel himself. So the only course was to cut the cylinder into three parts, which the ancient Assyrian and his fellow-priests had done, using two for Ninib's ear rings and disposing of the third where it would never be found. He suggested that Hilprecht place the two rings together and make due allowance for the missing third, thus completing the full inscription.

Waking suddenly from his fantastic dream, Dr. Hilprecht related it in detail to his wife, so that he would not forget it. The next morning, he pieced together the two fragments of agate and by filling in a missing third, he formed and translated the inscription:

TO THE GOD NINIB, SON OF BEL, HIS LORD, HAS KURIGALZU, PONTIFEX OF BEL, PRESENTED THIS

Efforts were made to explain this remarkable dream by assuming that all the essential facts were available to Dr. Hilprecht and that when they fell in line while he slept, he created the dream image of an ancient priest of Bel in order to account for them. Yet it is far more likely that a man as close to his subject as Dr. Hilprecht would have come to his final finding much more readily while awake. That leaves the bizarre alternative that back when the ear rings of Ninib were fashioned, an ancient pagan priest may have dreamed of traveling far into the future while a modern scholar was coming back through time in the same manner, resulting in the meeting of two minds that were actually more than three thousand years apart!

VI

Dreams and Crime

It has long been claimed that there is some subtle magnetic force that causes a murderer to return to the scene of his crime. This is similar to the saying that coming events cast their shadow before. If you put the two together, you will have a startling combination of forces, as the stories told in this chapter will prove.

The fact that some overwhelming compulsion can be carried from waking life into the dream urge is a strong indication that it can be projected further, even from one mind to another. Just as guilty persons have given themselves away by talking in their sleep, so may they divulge their secret schemes by broadcasting mental messages. This may take place before the crime, during its commission, or afterward.

The time element here is difficult to define, as such a thought chain may not be picked up or recognized until later. Also, there is no telling if it will reach the mind toward which the threat is directed. Often such mental broadcasts are registered by some disinterested party who happens to be tuned to the same telepathic wave length.

In contrast, there are cases where the threatened victim sends out the psychic cry of danger, frantically seeking a receptive mind already attuned to his own. Such instances are included in this chapter.

The Assassination Dream Though more than a century and a half has passed since the dream sequence now to be related occurred, it remains a standout, both because of the importance of the events involved and the thorough way in which it was attested. Morever, it carries a special impact in relation to our present-day world, when similar events are all too frequent and perhaps people are still too reticent to speak up when they have ominous dreams.

The tin and copper mines of Cornwall were working overtime in the year 1812, supplying England with wartime needs against Napoleon. The busiest man in that remote county was John Williams, the superintendent of several of the largest mines. By his own statement, Williams was far too busy to worry about politics or even pay any attention to changes in the British ministry. But on May 3rd, 1812, such matters were brought sharply to his mind when he had a very vivid dream which remained clearly etched when he awakened.

In the dream, Williams found himself in the lobby of the House of Commons in London, where he had been some time before on matters pertaining to the mines. He recognized the place by its four pillars marking the entrance to the House and a fireplace with benches, where visitors waited. Near one of the pillars was a man wearing what Williams later described as a "snuff-colored" coat, with large metal buttons, who stepped toward a small man, dressed in blue coat and white waistcoat, who had just entered the lobby.

As Williams watched helplessly, he saw the taller man bring a pistol from beneath his coat and fire it at the new arrival, who fell to the floor with blood staining his white waistcoat. Williams distinctly heard the shot and saw the color of the victim's face change as he lay motionless near the pillars. There was an immediate furore in which several men sprang forward and seized the murderer; then, Williams found himself asking who the victim was and heard someone answer, "Mr. Perceval, Chancellor of the Exchequer."

Waking suddenly from the nightmare, John Williams awakened his wife Catherine and described it to her. She took the attitude that it was "only a dream" and told him to go back to sleep, which he did. Soon he was having the same dream as before, complete in every detail. Again, he told his wife, took her advice to go back to sleep, and therewith had the identical dream a third time. Impressed by its recurrence, he gave up sleep for the night.

At breakfast, all John Williams could talk about was his dream. Since he had never seen Spencer Perceval, Chancellor of the Exchequer, he decided to tell the dream to friends who had seen him. They agreed that the description fitted Perceval perfectly and since the chancellor had recently become prime minister of the cabinet, it was very likely that he would go to the House of Commons to make an address there. That stirred Williams to the point where he was ready to take the stagecoach from Truro to London and warn the prime minister that his life was endangered by a fanatic, who should be found and placed in custody at once.

But when Williams mentioned this to his family and his subordinates at the mines, they begged him not to go, insisting that he himself would probably be branded as a fanatic and held for observation. They added that if anything was to happen, it would now be too late to avert it, so Williams gave up his plan. Anxiously, he watched for the arrival of the London papers all the next week, but they contained no news even remotely resembling his dream. Then:

On the evening of May 13th, Williams' son came galloping on horseback from Truro and announced: "Father, your dream has come true! Mr. Perceval was shot in the House of Commons two days ago. An account of it has come to Truro after the newspapers were printed."

The next day's journals confirmed the details exactly as

Williams had dreamed them, even to Perceval's attire and
that of the assassin, a bankrupt merchant from Liverpool
named Bellingham, who blamed the ministry for the failure
of his business. Bellingham was tried, found guilty and
hanged a week after the murder. During his brief trial,
eye-witness reports served further to establish the accuracy of the dream.

To clinch it completely, Williams happened to go to London several weeks later and purchased a newly released
print that he saw in a shop window. The artist's depiction,
according to a signed statement by Mr. Williams, "coin-
cided in all respects with the scene in the dream. The colors
of the dresses, the buttons of the assassin's coat, the white
waistcoat of Mr. Perceval, the spot of blood upon it, the
countenances and attitudes of the parties present were exactly what I had dreamed."

Since those were points that Williams had earlier told to
friends, these same friends passed them along to other persons, including some government officials. At their request,
Mr. Williams personally repeated the details of his dream
for the official record. That was when the particulars were
still fresh and could be verified by those to whom he had
recounted the dream prior to the assassination.

Over all the years, one thing has never been doubted in
this remarkable case: Its authenticity. It is positive fact
that John Williams, staid mining superintendent, not only
had, but recounted a dream such as he never had before or
afterward. What type of dream was it?

Because of its fulfillment, it stands as a prophetic dream,
which is further substantiated by the fact that it was recurrent, a common feature of many prophetic dreams. The
other alternative is that it was telepathic; that Bellingham, madly flashing his intended purpose from Liverpool
had his thoughts picked up by Williams in Truro. A question here: Since Perceval was the threatened man, why

didn't he receive Bellingham's sinister flash himself?

The answer is, he may have. Records show that for a week prior to the assassination, Spencer Perceval had strong premonitions of his own doom, though he could not explain it. He is said to have told his family and friends of these forebodings and he even made out his will because of them. But that brings up another factor: All that while, John Williams, in his home near Truro, was fighting off the overwhelming urge to speed to London on the fastest coach and warn the prime minister in person. It well could be that Williams was relaying telepathic flashes to Perceval who translated them as premonitions!

The Strange Case of William Terriss Early in the morning of December 16th, 1897, an actor named Frederick Lane had a very vivid and gruesome dream. Lane at that time was a member of the company in a melodrama called *Secret Service* which was playing at the Adelphi Theatre in London, England. The principal part was played by William Terriss, a 50-year-old actor who had formerly appeared in Shakespearian drama with Sir Henry Irving; and in the dream, Lane saw Terriss lying unconscious on a stairway back stage of the Adelphi.

Lane recognized other persons in the throng surrounding the stricken actor and all were trying to help him. What had caused the scene, Lane could not guess, but he was sure that something serious had happened to Terriss and that the show would not go on that night. Late in the morning, Lane went to the theatre and related his dream in detail to five of the other actors, who were strongly impressed, but tried to treat it lightly rather than have it prey on their minds.

Terriss was not due at the theatre until shortly before show time, which was unfortunate, as it prevented him from hearing about Lane's dream. Actually, none of the actors wanted Terriss to hear about it, for since he was the apparent victim of the the dream, it could have disturbed him more than anyone else. But there was a reason why Terriss might have accepted that dream as a very significant omen, though Lane and the others knew nothing about it.

In recent months, Terriss had been hounded by an eccentric character actor named William Archer Prince, familiarly known as "Mad Archer." Terriss had charitably befriended Prince, because of old acquaintance and had given him money, only to have him demand more, using absurd pretexts to support imaginary claims. When Terriss flatly refused some of the fanatical demands, Mad Archer had become threatening and Terriss, rather than be annoyed further, had decided to avoid him and let him go his way.

Lane's dream might have caused Terriss to think in terms of Prince and class the man as more dangerous than harmless; but as it was, Terriss merely decided to come into the theatre by a side entrance instead of the regular stage door, as he knew that Prince might be waiting to accost him there. That evening, Prince was not only waiting outside, he was looking through the stage door and saw Terriss arrive by the other route. Madly, Prince dashed past the unsuspecting doorman, pounced upon Terriss as he reached the stairs leading up to the dressing rooms and stabbed him furiously with a long-bladed knife.

People backstage dragged the madman away too late. Someone rushed out shouting for a doctor and the first man to hear it was Frederick Lane, who was on his way to the theatre. Lane dashed to Charing Cross Hospital to get the doctor and then hurried back to the theatre. When he arrived backstage, he stopped, utterly shocked by the very scene that he had dreamed and described that same morning, almost to the exact detail. But now, Lane knew what it was all about. William Terriss had been stabbed to death.

The show did not go on that night, nor any other night, as it was immediately closed. William "Mad Archer" Prince went on trial for murder and was adjudged insane. The London *Times* of December 17th, 1897, the day after the murder, included the facts of Lane's dream along with the account of the crime. Within the next few days, a noted psychic investigator, Frank Podmore, interviewed Frederick Lane and persons to whom he had recounted the dream and they furnished him with affidavits as to its veracity.

Podmore classed the dream as a telepathic type. His theory was that Mad Archer, "brooding in solitude," had determined upon "a desperate purpose" which he could have localized as to time as well as place. That formed "the outline of a picture" which he could have "unawares communicated" to some mind like Lane's "which happened to be sensitive to its reception."

That theory is still good, and during the years since many other remarkable dreams have been recorded to support it. With the advent of ESP, investigators have probed much further into such possibilities and many have agreed fully with Podmore. It should be noted that Frederick Lane was the one actor in the cast of *Secret Service* who had rehearsed the leading role as understudy to William Terriss so their minds could have been so well attuned that Lane instead of Terriss, picked up the death threat projected by Mad Archer.

The Dream that Helped the Mounties George Hayward and his brother Edward were natives of Kent, England and both had taken to the sea, though after that, their careers differed. George worked his way up to captain of a Clan Line ship and finally retired from service and went back home to Kent. Edward had continued as a seaman until he reached Australia, where love of adventure had lured him on the trail of gold. After various ups and downs, he shipped to Canada, to try his luck as a prospector there.

Over the years, the brothers had corresponded at intervals, for there had always been a close bond between them. After Edward reached Canada, he wrote to George, saying that he was going north from Edmonton, Alberta. With the letter, Ted—as George always called him—enclosed a recent photograph of himself, which George showed to their sister and other relatives living in Kent.

That was in the summer of 1904. On September 17th, Captain George Hayward had a most unusual dream. He seemed to be moving through a vast expanse of wooded land with lakes and rivers, far different from anything that he had ever seen. His dreams, whenever he had them, were usually of the sea or rocky coasts, so when he wakened, he was more than puzzled; he felt as though he had actually come back from somewhere very far away and very strange.

When Captain Hayward went back to sleep, the dream was still sharp in his mind, for it picked up from where it left off. Now, however, he was closer to the scene, for it focused on a campsite beneath some overhanging trees. Moonlight flickered through the leaves and the glow from a fire revealed two men sleeping in rolled-up blankets. As Captain Hayward watched what seemed a real-life drama, one rose, drew a rifle from a stack of packs and approached his sleeping companion, whose face was suddenly revealed in the trickly moonlight.

It was the captain's brother Ted, wearing a black beard as shown in his photograph! Staring helplessly, Captain Hayward saw the other man raise the rifle and fire it at Ted's head. As Ted's body writhed, the killer fired again and Ted sank lifeless in the blankets. With that, the dream drama faded.

In the morning, Captain Hayward dismissed his dream

experience in hearty style. He laughed at the notion that brother Ted would let himself be calmly murdered after so many years before the mast and in the Austrailian bush. Obviously, Ted's bearded picture, his letter saying that he was going north, had stimulated Captain Hayward into taking an imaginary voyage of 6,000 miles and the same distance back, all in one night's dream, with the incidents mere nightmare stuff.

The more the captain talked in that light-hearted way, the more the story of his dream impressed the family, then his friends, and finally a reporter from the local newspaper, who interviewed him a few days later and printed an exact account of the dream. That would have marked the end of it, except for certain things which were happening in the Canadian province of Alberta at that very time.

There, the chief of a local Indian tribe paddled into a place called Buffalo Bay to talk to the sergeant of a Royal Canadian Mounted Police detachment that was stationed there. The chief said that two prospectors had camped near his reserve for a few nights, but that one had left, taking along horses loaded with packs. The other man, who was tall and wore a black beard, had apparently gone his own way without any equipment, or even his dog, for a black collie that had been with the campers refused to follow the man who took along the pack train.

Suspecting foul play, Sergeant K. F. Anderson of the RCMP began an intensive investigation. Examination of the campsite showed that the fire had been an unusually large one and fragments of bone were found in the ashes, while poplar leaves that wavered from overhanging boughs showed traces of grease that could have come from burning fat. Anderson put Indians to work scouring the marshy terrain and they came up with trifling clues, one an empty coin case of a type used to hold English gold pieces. The maker's name was stamped on it, with a number, so Anderson sent it to England in hope that its owner could be traced.

At Athabasca Landing, Sergeant Anderson caught up with the pack-train man who gave his name as Charles King and said that the missing man was a stranger who had camped with him one night and then left. King was held on suspicion while Anderson and other Mounties checked back along the trail and found that the black-bearded man, far from being a stranger, was obviously King's partner, for many witnesses had seen the two together.

Steadily, the chain of circumstantial evidence was forged against King. The horses were traced to a dealer who said that it was the black-bearded man who had paid for them and that he was either an Englishman or an Australian. A harness-maker remembered the same man buying saddles and other equipment. A settler at whose place the men had stopped thought they had referred to each other as "Charley" and "Ted"; but although the "Charley" could mean King, he still stuck to his story that his companion was a stranger. As for the nickname "Ted," that wasn't enough for the investigators to go on.

What they needed was the full name and identity of the supposed victim, documentary evidence that he had gone North to prospect with a partner, and above all, an actual witness to the murder. Suddenly, all three came from a single source. The manufacturer of the English coin case had checked its number and found that it had been sold long ago to an elderly man named Hayward, whose son George was a retired sea-captain now living in Kent, so he had been contacted.

Captain Hayward recalled that his father had given the coin case to his other son, Edward, whom everyone called Ted. He sent Ted's latest picture on to the Mounties and with it, Ted's letter from Edmonton, telling of his plans.

From that, investigators gained new leads that practically clinched the case against Charles King, and soon afterward, Captain George Hayward arrived in Edmonton in person. With him, he brought the newspaper account of the dream which he now knew had actually symbolized his brother's murder.

The dream tallied with the crime, both as to time and place, as well as the participants. The description of the scene was exact in detail, even to the flickery moonlight, the sort that the rustle of poplar leaves would induce. Though the dream could not be introduced as evidence— though today, many people feel that such dream should be!—it formed the blueprint for the scene as the investigators reconstructed it at the trial. Charles King was found guilty of murdering Edward Hayward and was hanged on September 30th, 1905.

The Log of the Orient The amazing case of Captain George Hayward and his brother Edward brings home two vital points, where dreams are concerned. One is the natural affinity between two persons who are closely related, in that case, brothers. The other is that someone whose life is isolated or lonely—which applies specifically to a sea captain —should naturally be susceptible to impressions projected from afar, because his very isolation puts him in a receptive mood.

In the Hayward case, George, the retired sea captain, could well have been dreaming what was happening to the folks at home. So naturally his dream life was attuned to his brother Edward, who was experiencing, in his own way, the very adventures that George would still have relished.

But suppose it had been turned entirely about. Assume that a sea skipper, tossing far out on the deep blue sea, should think of his brother, solidly fixed at home, and wish that he could be there, too, only to discern that real danger lay there!

This can best be appreciated by telling it exactly as it happened and was duly recorded; to wit:

On February 8th, 1840, Nevill Norway, a merchant of Whitebridge, Cornwall, rode on horseback to the town of Bodmin and transacted some business in gold and silver, which were both current in those days. This was observed by a young man named William Lightfoot, who promptly contacted his brother James. Together they waylaid Mr. Norway, while he was riding home on horseback at half-past ten that evening.

For what happened next along that road in Cornwall, England, we turn to the log of the sailing ship *Orient*, which had rounded the Cape of Good Hope on a return voyage from the Phillipine Islands. The ship was commanded by Edmund Norway, a brother of Nevill; and on February 9th, Captain Norway added the following statement to his log of the day before:

Ship *Orient*, from Manilla to Cadiz: Feb. 8th, 1840.

About 7:30 p.m. the island of St Helena, N.N.W., distant about seven miles, shortened sail and rounded to, with the ship's head to the eastward; at eight, set the watch and went below—wrote a letter to my brother, Nevill Norway.

About twenty minutes or a quarter before ten o'clock, went to bed, fell asleep and dreamt I saw two men attack my brother and murder him. One caught the horse by the bridle and snapped a pistol twice, but I heard no report; he then struck him a blow and he fell off the horse. They struck him several blows and dragged him by the shoulders across the road and left him. In my dream there was a house on the left-hand side of the road.

At five o'clock (Feb. 9th) I was called and went on deck to take charge of the ship. I told the second officer, Mr. Henry Wren, that I had had a dreadful dream and dreamt that my brother Nevill was murdered by two men on the road from St. Columb to Wadebridge; but I was sure it could not be there, as the house there would have been on the right-hand side, but it must have been somewhere else.

He replied, "Don't think anything about it; you West-country people are superstitious; you will make yourself miserable the remainder of the passage." He then left the general orders and went below. It was one continued dream from the time I fell asleep until I was called at five o'clock in the morning.

Edmund Norway
Chief Officer, Ship *Orient*

In Cornwall, first inkling that Nevill Norway had been murdered came when his gray horse arrived home riderless with bloodstains on its saddle. Searchers backtracked along the route and the next day found the brutally bludgeoned body of Nevill Norway in a brook where the killers had dragged it. The victim's purse had been taken and the broken hammer of a pistol was found near the scene of the crime. Suspicion gradually centered on the Lightfoot brothers and when they were arrested, the broken pistol was found in their possession.

James Lightfoot admitted aiming the pistol at Nevill Norway and pulling the trigger twice, but it had missed fire. William had then struck the victim with a club, knocking him from his horse and James had battered him with the pistol until it broke. So when Captain Edmund Norway arrived home from sea, he was amazed to learn that his dream of his brother's murder had been correct in every detail.

Yes, in every detail. For when Captain Norway went to view the actual scene, he found that during his long absence, the road from Bodmin had been improved and the house that he remembered as being on the right, was now on the left side of the road, exactly as in his dream!

VII

Dreams Dictionary

From antiquity onward, many dreams have been regarded as symbolic, the main question being how far such symbolism might go. Three factors determined the significance of such dreams: The interpreter, the dreamer, and the times. Early interpreters were primitive, but so were the dreams that they interpreted; so, also were the times in which the dreamers lived. Hence they were more generally right than wrong.

As life became more complex, so did dreams and therefore their interpretations. But those seldom were hit-or-miss, for the interpreters had many cases to draw from and were prompt to provide new meanings when changing times demanded them. It took our modern analysts, however, to recognize how deep-set or totally disguised certain symbols might become.

That was particularly true with dreams involving sex. Hence Dr. Sigmund Freud, in dealing with sex-repressed patients, interpreted almost all dream impressions as sex symbols, male or female. Freud's list would be superfluous as anybody can make one up with very little imagination. Later analysts were broader in their views, interpreting dream symbols in terms of other repressions that come under a more general listing.

To these add traditional interpretations that still are recognized, including those that link with ancient myths or creeds that have a continual influence in the world of dreams. Give due place to dreams of an inspirational nature, as noted by Edgar Cayce, the famous "sleeping prophet" and others who favor such interpretations. Make due allowance for dreams which may seem contradictory, like the natures of the dreamers themselves, and the scope will become still broader and even more intriguing, as the following alphabetical list will prove:

Abyss: We start with "abyss" because it forms a standby from the ancient dream books when any engulfing depth was termed an "abyss." To dream of one meant threats of losing property, personal quarrels and unwelcome cares. In a modern list of psychoanalytical interpretations we find the same term included as denoting lack of self-confidence in business, love and any of life's problems. To fall into a deep pit proves that you have already accepted failure. This is one case where old and new interpretations are quite close.

Accident: This was once interpreted as a warning not to take a journey for the next week or fortnight as it might prove dangerous. Today, when travel not only is a necessity but represents a calculated risk before you even start, such advice would be hard indeed to heed. One modern interpretation treats an accident as symbolizing that someone is trying to interfere with your plans, which might mean that you would have to travel soon, far and fast to get ahead of them—quite the opposite of the old notion. There is also a psychic interpretation; namely, that you will at least see or hear of an accident within the next few days, so be on the watch for one to make sure it does not apply to you. If you see one, the pressure is off.

Acrobat: This is an old warning of risk that may involve you personally. Today many hazardous schemes require good judgment on your part lest your own plans be thwarted. Be alert for an imminent change that may be harmful to you especially if you fall or see another acrobat falling.

Actor, Actress: When you dream you are acting it is generally accepted that you are in need of recognition of your talent. A more modern interpretation is that you are depending too much on the wrong people.

Adhesive Tape: To dream about adhesive tape denotes an effort to hide something or that you have a secret that you do not wish exposed.

Airplane: While this is a type of travel dream, it also expresses a person's desire to be up to date and modernize all his activities. In short it is the dream of a "go-getter." However this should not be confused with specialized airplane dreams. A crash would come under the term of accident, while missing a plane would be a frustration dream. An old obsolete plane would represent disappointment or dissatisfaction with present connections. Refer "Accident," "Travel," "Missing the Boat," page 51, and "Interrupted Preparation," page 52.

Alley: If it is a narrow alley it falls into the category of tight place dreams. By old interpretations, if it appears as a passageway, vexing problems need much consideration on your part. If very narrow (tight place) one theory places this as a sexual craving. Refer "Being Trapped in Tight Places," page 51.

Alligator: An alligator has always meant trouble. At best it signifies caution while dealing with people.

Almond: Traditionally the almond has always been considered lucky but like its bitter taste sorrow may accompany any acquisition of wealth. Hence it warns of possible disappointment.

Anchor: This was always considered a good sign for sailors. Nowadays it is a key to settle down in one spot, such as in your occupation or your home.

Angel: Long a token of personal desires for happiness, it remains a symbol of love and a warning to transgressors. It can show a need for protection.

Animals: Pets have always meant satisfaction to the dreamer, but if an animal is suffering, the dreamer may be called upon for assistance either to an animal or a person. Modern sources consider a dream of a wild animal as a sex symbol.

Ants: Ants are always considered to be a symbol for worries. Just small annoyances that the dreamer may tolerate but must dismiss.

Ape: Deception still holds for this symbolic creature. Double dealing by someone known to the dreamer.

Apples: A good sign if on the tree or ripe and luscious looking. The modern trend is to consider the apple as a source of sexual temptation reverting to the Garden of Eden with a Freudian interpretation—rounded like a woman's breasts. Depending upon the dreamer, the old adage "an apple a day keeps the doctor away" could be applied. Not everyone is filled with the sex problem, nor neurotic.

Arrow: The arrow, being long and pointed, is considered as a Freudian sex symbol, a sign for passionate love. Cupid's bow and arrow, long signifying love, falls into this same dream interpretation.

Automobile: Many dreams with automobiles are a definite warning. The authors have had many such dreams and either they are a personal warning or one that points to an accident for other people. Cayce cited incidents of this sort and his words were those of admonishment for the dreamer. If the car is speeding or moving along, the dream can be interpreted in the Freudian manner if the reader wishes to do so. Many dreams that simply involve an ordinary auto should come under the heading of travel, however the mode of travel is very important. Automobile dreams, for example, may be the equivalent of the old horse dreams.

Ax: Self-reliance and struggles that are necessary to obtain security have long been the meaning of the ax dream. If broken, advancement may be slow.

Baby: A baby signifies happiness for the dreamer; if crying, unhappiness might follow. Generally we accept the interpretation of innocence and the chance to start something new and fresh. To give birth indicates a sexual urge.

Ball: A ball, as in a game, predicts an interest in a sporting event. If the dream is about a festive ball with dancing it signifies an ambition not yet achieved. If the ballroom scene produces sadness or disappointment, frustration, bad news may come to the dreamer. The ball also symbolizes the breast of a woman.

Balloon: The balloon is a sex symbol by today's standards.

Banana: This is a warning not to overindulge the appetite. Refer "Food and Eating," page 00.

Bank: A dream of a bank implies that the dreamer has many worries. Many packages of bills, a chance to get an unexpected sum of money.

Bartender: This dream represents conviviality. That the dreamer is looking for someone in whom to confide, that is unless it is an excuse for going on a binge.

Bath, Bathing: This is a sex dream of projection, though in olden days it applied to domestic problems. It can also be applied to a business clearing, inventory and the like that require time consuming, lengthy hours of work like cleaning house.

Battle: A battle complex of any kind shows a troubled mind. Your inner nature is fighting against itself.

Bats: This is a flying dream but always indicates fear of something, or of unpleasant news. Refer to "Flying Through the Air," page 47.

Bayonet: The bayonet means fear of an opponent. It is also a male sex symbol.

Beach: This is considered a water dream. It is a desire to escape for relaxation. Sometimes it stands for sexual relations even though the dreamer may never have had a sexual experience.

Bed: To see a bed as in a store display means that a surprise awaits you. If you dream that you

DREAMS   *102

are in a bed different from your own you should make new
friends or seek new opportunities to express yourself. If the
bed is made, you need more security. If unmade, frustration
is ahead. A sick person in the bed means trouble for that
person and perhaps yourself.

Bedroom: This is a desire for something new. It
is also rated as a significant impulse for sexual implications.

Bees: Formerly considered a warning of
troublesome worries, especially if the bees swarm and sting.
Buzzing bees promise an increase in profits or a turn for the
better in business and home economy.

Beggar: The beggar dream denotes small problems, or an economic struggle that must be improved. A
hand-out to a beggar brings a pleasant surprise for the
dreamer.

Bells: Bells that toll announce a death. Any
other bells promise good news for the dreamer.

Berries: Picking berries denotes varying problems and vexations that disturb you. Eating berries can be
lucky sign of financial gain. Blackberries are the most ominous. Strawberries alone are a good omen of joy and
devotion.

Betting: If betting on races in the dream, be
careful in business transactions; losses may be near. If at
gaming tables, beware of tricky schemes.

Bicycle: If riding a bicycle uphill, cheerful
events are due. If riding downhill, it can be losses or a mis-
hap. The bicycle is also a sex symbol.

Bigamy: This is a warning to be discreet and keep your sensual emotions under control.

Billiards: Playing billiards indicates a need to overcome uncertainty. Seeing an empty billiard table hints at unseen people who are causing you much annoyance.

Birds: Caged birds mean unhappiness or sorrow for the dreamer. If the birds are in flight you will prosper by a change. It can also be interpreted as a desire for sexual escape. To kill a bird is bad luck for the dreamer. Birds of prey mean sadness. To see many birds augurs legal entanglements or gossip. A singing bird promises ecstacy. A bird flying against a window, as if trying to enter, usually brings news of a death of someone close to the dreamer.

Bird's Nest: If you see an empty nest, you will meet with opposition. If eggs are in the nest, a profitable negotiation is in sight. With young birds, the dreamer is due for a change or travel.

Birthday: If you dream that you are having a birthday it is a desire to release emotional strain. If you receive presents, it is a struggle to evade pressing responsibilities.

Blindness: If you are the blind one you need a change of environment. If you see a blind person someone needs your care and love.

Blindfold: The blindfold dream is a signal of distress; inability to make decision.

Blood: To see blood usually means bad luck

for yourself or someone close to you. Blood-stained clothes show aggressiveness that can be dangerous to self and others. Bleeding indicates viscious impulses that should be controlled.

Blossoms: A dream of blossoms augurs a turn for better times.

Boa-constrictor: The snake, synonymous with venom and hatred, becomes a multiple threat with the boa-constrictor, meaning enemies that cause the dreamer much confusion. Snakes of all kinds are considered sex symbols.

Boat: A boat or a ship means that the dreamer would like a change. It is also a prediction that something pleasant is about to happen.

Bomb: Disturbances, such as arguments at home, in daily routine, as in business, whether personal or political, can send the dream mind into a dramatic, chaotic state so that a bomb mentioned in the news makes this a plausible reaction in the retrospective dream analysis. Such a dream serves as an outlet to repressed thoughts. It represents a temporary emotional unbalance that seems to need the shock of a bomb, which at once discharges anger and fear. To dream of a bomb has long meant many arguments. In modern life many loud noises may actually disturb the sleeper and rouse disturbed thought in the mind. In short, arguments in dreams are symbolic of a temporary emotional unbalance.

Books: Books naturally are a symbol that relate to the pursuit of knowledge, a need for something new, either entertaining or informative. Too many books lend an air of confusion; hence in recalling the dream a definite reason or relation must be sought for, that is, the kind of books, the owner, the subject matter, such as text books, old books as in a secondhand shop, library, or church. If the dream is one of vagueness like staring at empty book-cases, look for an new interest. If in a bookstore you may see exactly what you want, this may mean that you already have too many interests that are impeding your progress. There is also the possibility of a desire to search for the answer to a secret buried deep in the subconscious. For centuries books symbolized knowledge but with the modern deluge of reading they are more apt to represent escape. If Freud were around today and could read some of our literature, particularly those with pictures, he would be justified in giving books a sexual inference.

Boss: A change may be due in your affairs.

Bow and Arrow: This is a symbol for love as in Cupid's bow and arrow and this ties in with the Freudian theory of the subconscious call for sexual relationship.

Box: An unopened box has a two-fold mean-ing in that you have a secret or that you are anticipating something new such as a gift. An empty box suggests that you must find new sources of work. The box is sometimes classified as a sex *motif* pertaining to women.

Bracelet: The bracelet dream pertains to sex and means news of a wedding which can be your own or some-one else's. If you find a bracelet unexpected assets or val-uables may soon be received. Today the shape, being round, refers to the sexual organs of a woman.

Bread: An old interpretation of a dream about white bread means increased wealth for the rich but a loss for those who are poor. Dark bread signifies the reverse.

Bride: For a girl to dream that she is a bride once meant that she would come into money or have very good luck, but if she were displeased with the wedding arrangements the whole ceremony would be tinged with disappointments. You would expect modern dream analysts to come up with more complicated conclusions than that. Instead, some of them solemnly announce that a bridal dream is obviously an undisguised wish fullfillment, denoting love, sex or marriage and possibly all three.

Bridegroom: Same as bridesmaid

Bridesmaid: This is a wish fullfillment dream associated with a fear complex that it may never happen or a basic sex element that is naturally associated with marriage.

Brush: To dream of an old brush in olden days meant ill health; a new brush, a need for a new interest; clothes brushes or an assortment of brushes, too many tasks at one time may be hindering the dreamer.

Bugle: A bugle call to arms, to work or a call to rest is a likely dream for the serviceman, but to the average person unattached to such organized groups or musical organizations the sound of the bugle predicts fortunate and happy events, without imposed restrictions. It is also included as a phallic symbol along with other pointed objects.

Bugs: Like ants, bugs represent many little irritating problems. Edgar Cayce referred to them as a warning of bad conditions surrounding the dreamer.

Buildings: Dreams of large tall buildings infer that the subconscious self is desirous of travel to new places. At the same time moderns call this another phallic symbol perhaps adding strength while making a decision.

Bull: Usually a bull indicates a warning of harrassment for the dreamer though the white bull of India is an omen of higher achievement pertaining to the mind and spiritual sense as opposed to the physical. It can also represent a person who is a poseur, one who obviously has a lively imagination bordering on the extravagant, hence unreliable.

Burglar: For women the burglar represents a sex motif especially since burglars are usually armed. In any case the burglary is a fear that something is about to be stolen or lost; sexually it means the loss of virginity.

Burial: Dreams of burials have long been given contradictory explanations such as happiness, good health or marriage, while contrary to these predictions are sickness, adversity and depression. Cayce considered some aspects of a dream of death as a shaking off or elimination of a mental attitude in order to replace it with a new and better one. Where the dreamer is being buried alive, self-imposed punishment serves to exonerate the conscience for a real or imaginary misdeed. If the self-burial dream is repetitious, it denotes great unhappiness with a desire for suicide rather than facing actualities.

Bus: This is a dream of travel. See Airplane; automobile; "Missing the Boat," page 51.

Butterflies: By some old interpretations, butterflies indicate inconstancy; by others, happiness and prosperity, especially for the very young. If in flight, butterflies mean good news from someone far away.

Buttons: Finding a button in a dream portends small gratuities. Losing a button is a warning of impending embarrassment, although slight. "Losing your buttons" has long been used as a catch phrase intimating forgetfulness. New trends associate buttons with the female sphere.

Cab: This is a moving enclosure which may be a sexual dream, but it deals with secretiveness and the urge to get to a definite goal. If there is more than one person in the cab, there is something that the dreamer wishes to establish for a personal whim or toward the exclusion of the other person or persons in the cab.

Cage: A cage, like a box, indicates a fear complex that may not be justified, but to be closed in a box is a dread of something much bigger than self. If a bird is in the cage it has long been considered an omen of an emotional strain. If the bird flies out of the cage, a liaison is imminent. Contrary interpretations long ago said luck was leaving you and a yoke would take its place.

Cakes: Dreaming of a cake can be just plain indigestion, but the proverbial wedding cake is for hopeful as well as disappointed lovers, meaning that frustration is the answer. Small cakes and cookies augur small emoluments. Traditionally, cakes mean contentment in business and a happy social life.

Candles: Candles in a dream just as in waking hours are a source of joy. The lighted candle signifies contentment. Burning at both ends means a desire to spend money or get a task done quickly. It shows a rebellious nature with a desire to prove other people wrong. It is said that for a young married woman it presages the birth of a beautiful child. If a lighted candle fades out, bad news is due. Moderns include the candle as a male sex symbol, marking it as strength or weakness in relation to the amount of light.

Candlesticks: The empty candlestick represents an imminent loss. Seven candlesticks as related in the Bible portray a spiritual interest that should be followed and developed in order to achieve success.

Cards: As in fortune telling cards and games, the ace of spades is the death or bad luck card. So it holds in dreams. Diamonds for money; clubs, ill will; hearts for love and friendship. Playing a game of cards for money forbodes a disagreement with one or more persons.

Cat: Cats have always been symbolic both of good and bad luck, and confusing though it be, the "good" and the "bad" have been applied to both black and white cats depending upon the interpreter. Since the cat is both a protective and destructive animal the dreamer must find some connection with the surroundings and the events in the dream before coming to a definite conclusion. The cat has long been the symbol of a woman by the popular term of "cat" or "catty." It is said that women who do not like cats have sexual problems, so in this case the dream of a cat may be a very personal warning to direct their emotional tensions in another direction. An attacking cat means enemies; a thin cat, bad luck for a friend; a scratching cat, difficulties that the dreamer must overcome.

Cave: Like the Abyss, a cave presents adversity in financial matters and sometimes in domestic channels, too. It is advisable to look around and see what can be done to avoid failure. Carl Jung classed the cave dream as the base, animal nature of man.

Chase: Refer to "Being Chased or Hunted," page 49.

Church: The church has long been symbolic of the spiritual state of the devoutly religious. If a church is being constructed it implies that divine love resolves the dreamer's dilemma. However if the church is in darkness, a state of melancholy needs enlightenment. To those in love, a chapel or church is the desire for marriage or a union that should be a lasting one. To those in distress this dream is a craving for protection.

Climbing: According to Freud any kind of climbing in any place indicates a desire for sexual relations.

Clock: To dream of a clock means impatience and worry, though a clock in a tower may signify a rise to power. If the clock is stopped it forbodes disappointment. Some people regard a striking clock as a sign of death to someone close to the dreamer.

Clothing: Refer to "Insufficient Clothing," page 54.

Cock: A crowing rooster in the early morning hours has always been the harbinger of a pleasant day; however at later hours the crowing is a warning to hold to truthfulness rather than deception. Likewise a cockfight means quarrels. Some analysts interpret the cock as a symbol of sexual infidelity.

Coffin: The coffin has dual interpretations. For some it signifies bad luck; to others it is good luck. A corpse in one, a marriage; yourself in the coffin, bad luck ahead, perhaps chagrin. Freudian followers look upon the coffin dream as a male sexual organ. The corpse then offers personal implications.

Coins: Gold coins that trickle through your hands indicate prosperity that should result because of your personal achievement. Silver coins are not so good, but if they are shiny your finances should be augmented. Copper and nickel portend unwieldy problems.

Crying: Crying is often a release of the emotions as in the conscious state. Being sorry for self or others is sometimes interpreted as a destructive element when the dreamer is failing in business or love.

Cutting: Cutting can be a desire to sever a business or personal connection. It is an emotional burden that must be resolved in spite of pride. If the cutting involves hair of the head or a beard it means, according to an old translation, persuasiveness in an ensuing argument or serious discussion. To see a cut warns the dreamer of illness or double-dealing by friends.

Dagger: Being pointed, the dagger falls into the category of a male sex symbol. In old dream analogy, a dagger or knife meant enemies are very near. If you throw the dagger or knife you must guard against hatred. If you take the dagger from someone's hand, you will overcome your enemies and attain your goal. According to some interpreters the dagger means the sex urge for men and women, but for women it may be a violation of a moral code.

Dancing: Considered by old standards, dancing is a dream of small pleasantries and happiness. To Freudian followers, dancing is a direct desire for sexual relations, depending on the dreamer or the persons included in the dream.

Danger: Refer to "Impending Danger." Also "Being Trapped In a Tight Place," page 51.

Death: To dream of dying implies that the dreamer wishes to escape from something or someone; that it is easier to die than face reality, or at least to seek a change. There are conflicting meanings to this type of dream in that the opposite of death means birth, joy and revelling, so the dreamer must make a decision by considering other facts of the dream, such as the place, the people and any activity concerned with it. Brides are known to have dreams of death which undoubtedly can be attributed to a change which calls for a lifetime of devotion and often servitude, even though they are not aware of it. To hear a dead person speak is usually a warning about a personal conflict.

Devil: A symbol of evil at all times, the presence of the devil indicates an inevitable guilt complex of the dreamer, especially if sex is complicated in waking hours. The subconscious serves in this case to carry on the mental stigma of conscious self, which means despair and consequent frustration.

Dog: Dog dreams have always had dozens of interpretations, depending on what the dog is doing. One modern interpretation symbolizes a dog as representing "animal ego" on the part of the dreamer. This fits with an old notion that to dream of a small dog means frivolous pleasures; snarling dog, trouble and quarrels; and a fine, big dog, wealth. If the dog attacks, misfortune or financial losses are imminent. A baying dog predicts scandal that involves the dreamer. A white dog predicts great happiness or a marriage. A black dog, by old translators, means deceit or fraudulent dealing by a friend or business connection. Often a dog may represent a person. Cayce said when you have a dog dream, look for an unfriendly relationship with someone.

Door:　　　　A door by Freudian terms is considered a symbol for the female sex, as if it were an entrance. However, by old or new divination, the closed door is a desire to go through to find something such as a secret and since the door is closed the dreamer meets with frustration. If open the signal for entrance is given and apparent satisfaction is inevitable to whatever the dreamer desires. To see others pass through a door means a change is in store for the dreamer.

Drinking:　　　　A sign of conviviality, the dreamer who is drinking is really looking for some mode of escape from surroundings in daily life. To watch others drinking indicates the dreamer is disgusted with companions or associates. This dream is also associated with the fact that the dreamer actually is thirsty and may wake up only to find it is true.

Driving:　　　　It is not uncommon for people who drive a great deal to find themselves driving in their dream life; however it can be a wish for self-importance or to be independent of others. If the driving is really racing, the dreamer wants to obtain something that requires risk, even hazardous gambling. If another person is driving, the dreamer will find assistance for a plan that is not yet completed.

Driving without being able to control the brakes means in-decision on the part of the dreamer, or lack of self-control, sometimes fear of responsibilities.

Drowning: Drowning usually means a loss of property or a person close to the dreamer. If rescued, the dreamer is on the way to advancement or relief from pres-ent pressure. To see another drown denotes bad news or a wish to see someone out of the way of the dreamer.

Eagle: A bird of prey, the eagle is powerful and dangerous; so, to the dreamer, when an eagle is in flight overhead, it is a warning of conflict, but success is to follow. Wealth and public acclaim are predicted when the eagle is perched high in a tree. It is said that killing an eagle in a dream is a sign of the fulfillment of the dream-er's ambition; however, if other people are involved in the killing, then the reverse is due for the dreamer. Cayce stated that the eagle is a symbol of love that is true and responsible for any subsequent duties. With children the eagle in a dream is a seeking for love even though they are not yet old enough to bear responsibilities.

Eating: Dreams of eating should refer to diet, that is, whether the diet should be modified or changed. Eating by oneself denotes a yearning for companionship to ward off melancholy or loneliness due to a loss of some sort. Eating with others foretells that a new friendship will soon be made or that the dreamer will have a monetary gain. Continuous eating warns the dreamer to let up on the daily strain of overwork or worry.

Elephant: The elephant, symbol of wealth, honor and power, is a good omen as long as the elephant does not trample upon the dreamer. In this case every precaution must be taken to avoid great losses. To feed an elephant indicates that the dreamer will enjoy new friendships through kindness and sympathy. Many elephants in a dream show a desire for power which will result from increased effort especially with the aid of a good memory. A newer interpretation places the elephant in a sex category where sexual frustration causes the dream.

Elevator: Any movement that is ascending or descending means, according to analysts, the desire of the dreamer to participate in sexual relations. Since the mechanized elevator is so important in modern living, the sexual interpretation seems likely. It is natural to assume that the rising elevator is significant of a desire to improve or increase the dreamer's position in life. If descending, the reverse is in order, and in turn implies chagrin and despair over some matter activated during the conscious hours. If the elevator stops between floors and does not move, dissatisfaction is evident and a change is wanted in home life or business connections.

Embrace: An embrace is a natural expression of affection and love. It is a sexual dream when it includes a sweetheart or lover. If the embrace is with a friend, members of the family, other than spouse, it means the dreamer would like to help that person.

Escape: To dream of escaping as if being chased means that you are trying to get more time to make a decision. If you do escape you will improve the situation. If you do not escape you will suffer embarrassment.

Examination: Refer to "Taking An Examination,"
page 52.

Falling: A very common dream is that of falling, which in itself is very frightening. It represents fear, the cause of which the dreamer must analyze and resolve to overcome. It can be a domestic or business problem, or for the young, fear of examinations or a wrong doing. For adults it can be a guilt complex because of immoral sexual relations. Refer to "Falling From a Height," page 46.

Father: An old translation of a dream about one's father is that subconsciously the dreamer needs his counsel and help. Modern analysts refer to it as a sexual symbol, one of vigor and power, going so far as to make it an Oedipus complex, which means there is a very strong link to the parent of the opposite sex and at the same time hatred of the other parent.

Fear: There are many types of fear dreams, but all are based on worry. Dreams of being attacked are common to women and associated with sexual actions. Old analysts merely considered a dream of fear as disappointment or frustration.

Fire: A dream of fire is usually favorable, promising an increase in finances and prosperity generally. At least a surprise is imminent for the dreamer. Another person in the dream predicts resentment. Refer to "Fire and Flame," page 56.

Fish: The fish, a symbol of life, traditionally meant that the dreamer would be favored by rich and powerful persons, especially if the fish is seen swimming around in a stream. To catch many fish, an increase in resources, good luck. If the fish is dead, a loss of money, bad luck. The ancients regarded two fish as a symbol of marriage and connubial bliss and modern interpreters swing back to that way of thinking by classifying the fish as a sexual symbol.

Flowers: Fresh pretty flowers signify unexpected pleasure. A bouquet refers to a wedding while a withered flower predicts sorrow and sadness. The daisy brings love; the rose, new admirers; lillies, frailty. Buds pertain to fertility and the need for love and family.

Flying: A dream of flying denotes ambition, a desire to achieve something worthwhile. An old interpretation was ominous, inferring that only calamity, illness or reverses were about to overwhelm the dreamer. Some moderns consider it a symbolic type of sexual desire that is subconsciously registering on the dreamer's mind. Refer to "Flying Through The Air," page 47.

Food: Refer to "Food and Eating," page 61.

Gambling: To win money gambling in dreams means loss of friends or money in waking life; to lose promises relief from troubles. These old concepts may have something for they conform to the Freudian idea of dreams representing opposites. Modern interpreters feel that the more you gamble in your dreams, the more risks or chances you will take. You might just wake up and find yourself in Las Vegas!

Garden: To cultivate or admire a garden means approaching good fortune. To walk in one, joy, especially dependent upon the person walking with you. But be sure it is a flower garden! Vegetables may signify misery or misfor tune. So does a neglected garden.

Goat: The goat is a symbol of sexual power

and in a dream it is a warning to keep the emotions under control. If you are riding a goat you may be involved in a scandal.

Gold: Like money, a dream of gold is the need for more wealth. The subconscious continues the struggle of the waking hours when the mind is directed toward gain and aspirations. If the gold is lost the dreamer has many inhibitions and fears and as such is likely to diminish the chance of increasing his financial status.

Grass: Grass is considered a lucky dream if the grass is fresh and green. It predicts an accumulation of wealth, success in business or profession, happiness in love. If the grass is withered, illness or business retardation may be near.

Gun: Since the gun is an instrument of violence it is held to mean the same n a dream. Like the dagger it is a male sex symbol.

Hair: Hair is associated with virility and sex. Many are the interpretations from ancient lore, such as to cut your hair means disappointment; tangled hair, business or family troubles; to see red hair, a change is near; long, beautiful hair, neglect because of vanity; to caress hair, you crave admiration and love.

Hat: Wearing a hat long indicates a change of business for the better and for a woman, the attainment of wealth and admiration. Freud made it an outright sex symbol and nothing else, but Jung swings toward tradition by classing it as a badge of power and dignity, like a crown or a halo. Secrecy is often the motif of a hat dream, tying it in with the old saying of "keep it under your hat."

Horse: Dreams of horses always have signified a rise in power or a gain of purpose, but with many variations. Literally there are dozens of interpretations that go back to the horse and buggy days when horses played an important part in everyday life. According to the old dream data, the color of horses like that of cats has dual contradictory meanings. The white and black horses mean both good and bad luck depending upon the dreamer's attitude. The bad luck is merely discontent. The good luck pertains to money or pleasure. Spotted horses predict better times. A wounded horse, trouble for the dreamer. The wild horse as an attacker is considered a desire for sexual relations if the dreamer is so minded. It means a fear of sex if a woman resents the act per se. The attacker and the fear analysis go along with the moderns who insist that horses represent a disguised sex urge. Oddly it may very well be that the dream of a horse simply means you like horses.

Hotel: Usually a hotel in a dream is the simple idea that the dreamer wants enjoyment and relaxation, a pleasant change or merely transient occupancy while transacting a business deal. The hotel is, by some, considered a motif for escape from a marital tie with sex as the ultimate motive.

House: Traditionally there are a few set interpretations about a dream of a house. If it is elegant or pretentious the dreamer wants something better than the present setting. To build a house means that you would do well to make a change. A dilapidated house is a bad omen that warns you to be careful of your business affairs and your health. Since a house is a symbol of our physical being, sex may enter into the meaning of the dream. In this case the part of the house and the poeple in it must be given due consideration.

Husband: For a wife to dream of her husband is a natural thing, but any variation from the normal provides a key to the subconscious even though the wife may not be aware of it. So, if she dreams that her husband is untrue to her, it indicates that she is jealous of him. If she is in love with another man in the dream, she is most likely unhappy with her husband. If she dreams that he is dead, she may actually wish him out of her life. If she dreams he is away from her, she really wants him close to her.

Island: To dream that you are on an island is a wish to escape from a disagreeable situation or you want to go away with someone you think you love. If there are people on the island, you crave more importance and feel that you must rise to something better. An island dream is a lucky sign that brings contentment that will come after you have worked out your desire or accomplished your ambition.

Jewels: Dreaming about beautiful jewels denotes an obsession for great wealth. To wear jewels, you are ambitious. If you receive a gift of jewelry, love and subsequent joy will come to you. If you lose jewels, be alert for theft or deception.

Jewelry: Same interpretation as Jewels.

Key: Any dream of a key indicates a desire for a change. Finding a key means unexpected good luck for the dreamer. A key is also considered a male sexual symbol so the interpretations apply to sexual relations.

King: The king, like the father, is the mark of authority, so if you dream of a king you may want to ask someone older than you for advice. If you dream you are a king, or a queen, you are very ambitious to control other people.

Knife: Like the dagger, the knife is a symbol of fear. It also symbolizes the male sex organ. Any complications in the dream involving quarrels and people should be given due consideration, because sex can actually be the cause of the irritation, jealousy, fear and even hatred.

Ladder: A ladder signifies that there is a strong urge to attain success and acknowledgement of work and talent.

Lock: The lock like the key indicates a change. To those in love a secret must be unlocked or revealed. Since the lock is looked upon as a symbol for the female sex organ the lock dream must be interpreted with sexual overtones. Refer to "Losing a Necessary Item," page 60, also "Being Lost," page 59.

Mask: The mask in itself means the concealment of a secret, deception or infidelity. If you dream you are wearing a mask it implies that you will be guilty of deception. If another person is wearing a mask that person is or will be guilty of fraud or deception. This is a common dream when infidelity exists and subsequent secrecy prevails.

Meals: See Eating; also "Food and Eating,"
page 61.

Mice: Mice and rats are fear symbols just as waking hours, for most people. In olden days a dream of mice warned the dreamer of personal and business difficulties, usually with a loss of money. The moderns classify mice and rats as a sex symbol, so an old interpretation about a young girl who dreams of mice, which meant scandal, would now mean sexual involvement ending in disgrace.

Money: To dream that you find money means that you want something more than you now have, such as a young fortune or a powerful position. To lose money, a purse or a wallet denotes a fear of financial loss or absolute poverty, total insecurity. To steal money presages financial problems. Refer to "Finding Money or Valuable Articles," page 48; "Losing Money and Valuable Articles," page 49. Also "Losing a Necessary Item," page 60.

Mother: Dreams about mother are numerous and recurrent from childhood to old age. Those that are pleasant are the happy continuation of the waking hours with her and need no implied significance. If you hear her calling you, it indicates neglect on your part. If you see her dead it infers you dislike her interference or advice. Children sometimes have this same dream, because they are afraid of losing her as their protector. To hear her crying means sorrow for you. Like the father dream, there can be an Oedipus complex.

Nakedness: Dreams of nakedness are subconscious form of exhibitionism; a desire to be noticed or to be more important. Even old significations express the same idea. One interpretation was that if you dream you are nude you secretly want to have "improper" relations with the opposite sex or, if you see another person naked, you may be tempted to participate in an immoral act because of bad associates. Today the implication is the same only more encompassing by adding homosexuality and similar sex deviations as a form of psychological regression to infantile desires like a child who wants to run around naked and show off. Refer to "Insufficient Clothing," page 54.

Nets: To be catching something in a net is a warning that the dreamer is unscrupulous in business or untrustworthy in love. If the net is torn you are on the brink of serious trouble.

Ocean: If the ocean is calm, your dream is prophetic of unexpected good fortune. If rough and stormy you have enemies who are undermining your efforts. If on a ship, you are anxious to be clear of your present responsibilities, so there must be something else that will give you occupational satisfaction. The ocean dream is a symbol of death or finality which in turn epitomizes the craving for a complete change, a new entity. Refer to "Water and Swimming," page 55.

Packing: The simple act of packing a suitcase or a trunk is an obvious dream that you would like to get away from it all. Very often you never get completely packed or you may not catch a bus or make airplane connections. This is a dream of frustration and bears a direct relationship to your waking status. Refer to "Interrupted Preparation," page 52.

Paralysis: The inability to walk, run, move your body or just to cry out while you are in a situation where you want to escape or ward off an attacker, puts you in a terrible state of panic. This is a dream of conflict and, due to the inability to cope with your conscious problems, the subconscious in the dream state only serves to magnify the dilemma. The relief upon wakening is tremendous and the realization that it was only a dream sometimes helps to alleviate the tension, though rarely can the dreamer remedy or reach a good solution.

Parents: See Father, Mother.

Pursuit: See Paralysis. Refer to "Pursuing Someone or Something," page 50.

Punishment: According to Wilhelm Stekel, M.D., noted psychologist, any form of punishment in a dream indicates a guilt complex, something that the dreamer might like to rectify, but hasn't.

Prostitute: According to Stekel, a dream wherein a man consorts with a prostitute, means that he is lacking sufficient sexual activity in his conscious hours. For a woman to dream that she is a prostitute implies that she craves sexual relations which are nonexistent in her conscious life. Stekel feel there is no disgrace in such dreams and that we profit by trying to understand them.

Rape: Similar to the prostitute dream, rape is the subconscious need to indulge in sexual relations whereby the woman dreamer is taken by force rather than willingly. Another interpretation is that the woman does not really want sexual fulfillment so in her dream world she becomes harrassed by an imaginary forced attack.

Rescue: Refer to "Rescuing Someone." page 58; "Being Rescued," page 59; "Being Lost," page 59; "Losing Some Necessary Article," page 60.

Rice: Dreams of rice have always symbolized marriage which is why throwing rice after the bride became a wedding ritual. Rice is a symbol of fertility.

Ring: Traditionally the ring has always been a token of love and friendship. In a dream it means a new friendship or even marriage. If the ring is broken, a loved one may leave you. Psychoanalysts classify the ring as a symbol for the female sex.

School: School dreams are common for young adults. This is often because of uncertainty over some coming project. Watch out for difficulties. Refer to "Taking An Examination," page 52.

Scissors: Scissors imply that quarrels are about to interfere with work. They are regarded as a sign of bad luck. Jealousy is usually associated with a scissors dream. See Dagger.

Stairs: Traditionally, stairway dreams mean approaching good fortune if you are going upstairs, bad luck if you are going down. Freud insists that either going up or down is symbolic of a sexual act. He includes ladders or any kind of steep incline, such as a mountain slope; even a piano because it has a scale. Jung felt that a downstairs dream meant encouragement.

Street: To dream of a long street, whether you are walking or running, indicates that you need a change or are implicated in a situation from which you wish to escape. Traditionally it all spelled worry. If it is a dead end street, the problems are confusing. If endless, you must find a new solution.

Swimming: Refer to "Water and Swimming," page 55.

Teeth: Refer to "Teeth," page 62.

Travel: Dreams of travel signify profit and pleasure unless the going is rough and difficult which may portend enemies and sickness. To travel alone is cause for worry. With a group, helpful companions. However the mode of travel is very important. Automobile dreams for example may be the equivalent of the old horse dreams. An airplane dream may be similar to the old train dreams. Refer to "Missing the Boat," page 51; "Interrupted Preparation," page 52.

Veil: To dream of wearing a veil may mean that you wish to hide something or that there is something you do not understand. If another person is wearing a veil, the implication may be deceit. A mourning veil, apart from sorrow, often means a threat of a financial loss. A bridal veil reflects something new that stirred the emotions during waking hours.

Walking: If the dream is about a path as in a wooded or rocky area petty worries are hounding you. If you are walking in darkness, fear is uppermost during waking hours. Refer to Street for "walking down a street."

Water: Traditionally a dream of water that is truly clear predicts prosperity; if muddy, a depressive period is near. Wading, playing or swimming in water indicates a sex urge or just a desire to be wanted. If the water is rough, your tasks may be overwhelming. If you are drinking water the chances are that you are actually thirsty. Nature functions even though we are sleeping! Refer to "Water and Swimming," page 55.

Zebra: Zebras have stripes so that they can hide in their native surroundings. The zebra dream implies there is a reason to hide either a truth or a lie. The zebra dream may also warn the dreamer that there is a situation that must be adjusted.

Zoo: To dream of a zoo denotes worry or confusion, depending upon the types of animals. If the animals are tame or quiet the dreamer may be finding a solution to a problem. If the animals are very wild or insecurely caged, real worries may become more serious.